Families
and
Communes

Understanding Families

Series Editors: **Bert N. Adams**, *University of Wisconsin*
David M. Klein, *University of Notre Dame*

This book series examines a wide range of subjects relevant to studying families. Topics include, but are not limited to, theory and conceptual design, research methods on the family, racial/ethnic families, mate selection, marriage, family power dynamics, parenthood, divorce and remarriage, custody issues, and aging families.

The series is aimed primarily at scholars working in family studies, sociology, psychology, social work, ethnic studies, gender studies, cultural studies, and related fields as they focus on the family. Volumes will also be useful for graduate and undergraduate courses in sociology of the family, family relations, family and consumer sciences, social work and the family, family psychology, family history, cultural perspectives on the family, and others.

Books appearing in **Understanding Families** are either single- or multiple-authored volumes or concisely edited books of original chapters on focused topics within the broad interdisciplinary field of marriage and family.

The books are reports of significant research, innovations in methodology, treatises on family theory, syntheses of current knowledge in a family subfield, or advanced textbooks. Each volume meets the highest academic standards and makes a substantial contribution to our understanding of marriages and families.

Multiracial Couples:
Black and White Voices
Paul C. Rosenblatt, Terri A. Karis,
and Richard D. Powell

Understanding Latino Families:
Scholarship, Policy, and Practice
Edited by Ruth E. Zambrana

Current Widowhood: Myths & Realities
Helena Znaniecka Lopata

Family Theories: An Introduction
David M. Klein and James M. White

Understanding Differences Between
Divorced and Intact Families
Ronald L. Simons and Associates

Adolescents, Work, and Family:
An Intergenerational Developmental
Analysis
Jeylan T. Mortimer and
Michael D. Finch

Families and Time:
Keeping Pace in a Hurried Culture
Kerry J. Daly

No More Kin: Exploring Race, Class,
and Gender in Family Networks
Anne R. Roschelle

Contemporary Parenting:
Challenges and Issues
Edited by Terry Arendell

Families Making Sense of Death
Janice Winchester Nadeau

Black Families in Corporate America
Susan D. Toliver

Reshaping Fatherhood: The Social
Construction of Shared Parenting
Anna Dienhart

Problem Solving in Families:
Research and Practice
Samuel Vuchinich

African American Children:
Socialization and Development
in Families
Shirley A. Hill

Black Men and Divorce
Erma Jean Lawson and Aaron Thompson

Romancing the Honeymoon:
Consummating Marriage in
Modern Society
Kris Bulcroft, Linda Smeins,
and Richard Bulcroft

The Changing Transition to Adulthood:
Leaving and Returning Home
Frances Goldscheider and
Calvin Goldscheider

Families and Communes:
An Examination of Nontraditional
Lifestyles
William L. Smith

William L. Smith

Families
and
Communes

An Examination of
Nontraditional Lifestyles

UNDERSTANDING FAMILIES

Sage Publications
International Educational and Professional Publisher
Thousand Oaks London New Delhi

For information address:

SAGE Publications, Inc.
2455 Teller Road
Thousand Oaks, California 91320
E-mail: order@sagepub.com

SAGE Publications Ltd.
6 Bonhill Street
London EC2A 4PU
United Kingdom

SAGE Publications India Pvt. Ltd.
M-32 Market
Greater Kailash I
New Delhi 110 048 India

Printed in the United States of America

Library of Congress Cataloging-in-Publication Data

Smith, William L., 1956–.
    Families and communes: An examination of nontraditional
lifestyles / by William L. Smith.
        p.   cm. — (Understanding families; v. 18)
    Includes bibliographical references and index.
    ISBN 0-7619-1073-5 (cloth: acid-free paper)
    ISBN 0-7619-1074-3 (pbk.: acid-free paper)
    1. Communal living—United States—History.   2. Collective
settlements—United States—History.   3. Family—United
States—History.   4. Alternative lifestyles—United States—History.
I. Title. II. Series.
HQ971.S55   1999
307.77′4′0973—dc21   99-6017

This book is printed on acid-free paper.

99   00   01   02   03   04   05   7   6   5   4   3   2   1

Acquiring Editor:	Jim Nageotte
Editorial Assistant:	Heidi Van Middlesworth
Production Editor:	Denise Santoyo
Production Assistant:	Patricia Zeman
Typesetter:	Lynn Miyata
Indexer:	Teri Greenberg

To the memory of my parents

Contents

Preface

While this book has been written primarily for a college audience, it will also appeal to those general readers who are interested in cultural issues such as family and community life, and religion. Students will find this to be a readable and enjoyable book that introduces them to the study of sociology and the social sciences by exploring the fascinating cultural diversity of nontraditional families and religious and secular communes or alternative communities. Instructors will see this as a cogent book that summarizes the scholarly literature on families and communities and introduces students to the concept of social order and a variety of groups such as the Hutterites, the Shakers, Oneida, Amana, the Mormons, and an array of modern rural and urban communes including Jesus People USA and Twin Oaks. Instructors will use this book as a supplement or as one of several main texts for courses in Family, Community, Religion, American and Cultural Studies, and Alternative Lifestyles. General readers, who acquire this book through their local library, bookstore, or via the Internet, will be introduced to the social scientific debate regarding family life, religious groups such as cults, otherwise known as new religious movements, and the direction of American society in the waning years of the twentieth century. Students, instructors, and general readers alike will find a lengthy bibliography that will help them facilitate further research on the topics and groups discussed throughout the book.

I wrote this book specifically to contribute to the ongoing debate among scholars regarding the role of family in community life. The primary thesis of this book is that families are an essential component of communal life. Most communes have not abolished the family. While this might be the case, many scholars believe that families often destroy or hinder communal living. We will investigate a variety of historical and contemporary communal groups to see how they dealt/deal with family life. For example, the Shakers abolished the nuclear family and were/are celibate, but they substituted what could be called a communal family for the nuclear family. Men and women, even former husbands and wives, looked upon each other as brothers and sisters. Selected elders and elderesses fulfilled the roles of parents or leaders. The Oneida Community practiced pantagamy, which is the belief that every man is married to every woman. The early Mormons and contemporary Mormon sects practiced/practice polygamy, otherwise known as plural marriage.

Communal groups are just one type of "nontraditional families," a label which embraces a wide range of family structural arrangements. The traditional nuclear family is no longer the dominant family form, and it behooves us to become familiar with some of the other types of families. This book focuses just on communal families.

We live in an era of fast-paced change, and our social institutions, especially the family, have been buffeted by social forces from both within and outside. The structural changes which have taken place in our families and communities did not occur overnight. They are embedded in the history of our country. The United States is one of the most diverse and pluralistic countries in the world, and we have always had nontraditional families and alternative communities present throughout our history. The attention given today to the issue of "family values" and the role of nuclear families is a perfect lead-in for studying nontraditional families and alternative communities. While some are calling for a return to the traditional nuclear family, others are venturing forth to create new ways of living in family and community. Some see family life focusing less on any prescribed arrangement or structure and more on intimacy and feeling and that which works for them.

Can communal families replace or substitute for the nuclear family? They can, but it is not easy or always successful. As we will discuss in the following chapters, some communes are predisposed to families while others are not. Amana resisted nuclear family life from a theological point of view, but they were pragmatists who realized they needed families to be a viable community. The majority of communes begun in the 1960s and 1970s were not predisposed to families, although many of them often referred to themselves as such. These utopians were much less concerned with developing new families and much more concerned with developing consensual community. Yes, some people did experiment with group marriage, but the vast majority did not. Even though we talk a lot about sex and we claim to have lived through several sexual revolutions, in the end our culture and society are still fairly traditional regarding sexual behavior.

We can learn much from communal groups about social order and conformity, change, our role as individuals in society, and the importance of balancing personal with community needs and wants. Join us on a journey which introduces us to families and communities you might not have known existed. What is their life like and what is important to them? Let them help us learn more about who we are by comparing and contrasting our lives with theirs. I wish I had had more space to share with you the history and the lives of other alternative communities and how they navigated the turbulent affairs of balancing family life with community life, but the groups presented here should whet your appetite and, I hope, broaden your understanding of our social life.

Acknowledgments

I have incurred many intellectual and personal debts while researching and writing this book. Most of all, I am grateful to David M. Klein and Bert N. Adams, editors of the Sage series, "Understanding Families." This book is as much a product of their keen insight and advice, as it is of my labor. I have benefited from the scholarship of Benjamin Zablocki, Rosabeth Moss Kanter, John Hostetler, and Donald Pitzer. I am very grateful for the unswerving support and encouragement of my colleagues Michael Delucchi and Peggy Hargis. I am appreciative of the assistance provided by the Department of Sociology and Anthropology, the Office of Research Services and Sponsored Programs, and the Zach S. Henderson Library at Georgia Southern University, as well as the Shaker Library at Sabbathday Lake, Maine. I accept full responsibility for the errors which, inevitably, were left undetected. Last, I am indebted to the men, women, and children who live communally. They are not only utopians, but they add to the richness and diversity of the human experience.

1

Introduction

Social Order and Personal Autonomy

If one is interested in the social scientific study of families and alternative lifestyles, what possibly could they learn from communes and intentional communities? Let us broaden the argument a bit further. What possibly could one learn about families and alternative lifestyles by looking at the various waves of utopian living the western world has experienced in modern times? What have groups like the Shakers, Oneida, Amana, and contemporary rural and urban communal utopias contributed to our understanding of family and community life?

Alternative lifestyles, such as communal living, provide us with additional models from which we can compare and contrast nuclear family life. Why would someone not want to conform to what everyone else is doing? What is it that motivates people to seek alternative family forms? These issues are important and warrant study because they aid us in understanding social solidarity and everyday life. Communal living provides its adherents something that many believe is missing in mainstream life. Modern life is frequently viewed as lonely and that mass society has eclipsed community, leaving us feeling fragmented and unattached to others (Slater, 1970; Stein, 1960).

American communalism made little impact on mainstream society until the latter part of this century (Kanter, 1977, p. 76). Although other communal scholars (see especially Pitzer, 1984a; 1984b; 1997a) will challenge her assumption, Rosabeth Moss Kanter is making a critical point. She is not dismissing the impact communalism and utopianism have had on the American psyche, but she is referring primarily to the lack of visible social structural changes in American society due to these processes. The major contribution communal utopias have made, according to Kanter (1977, p. 77), is in introducing mainstream society to new family forms. These new family forms are a harbinger of a movement toward, what Kanter describes as, the "postbiological family."

The terms *communes, intentional communities, communal utopias, communal societies,* to name a few of the many concepts used to describe communal living situations, 'are often used interchangeably. In most cases, they mean the same thing, which according to Donald Pitzer (1997a) includes, a place where property is shared, members join voluntarily, and share a belief system or ideology, and a lifestyle. There are variations of what these terms mean and Chapter 2 will highlight these differences, but for now this brief definition should suffice. Utopia is also a term that has many definitions, but for our purposes, utopias are places where people live as perfectly as they can while recognizing their limitations. Utopians are often referred to as social dreamers who are in search of a more perfect lifestyle.

What we can learn from communal utopias is how to bring a sense of community to family situations. Kanter (1977, p. 78) reminds us that communes are often short-lived and have other problems such as high turnover, but they are places of social experimentation where people try to create new and hopefully better intimate relationships. Communes are not replacements for families, but as Kanter (1977, p. 78) states, "Those biological families that wish to enrich the quality of their relationships can examine how communes go about intentionally creating a spirit of community."

A large number of communes and nuclear families, who have strong extended family ties, fail. Why is it so difficult for ordinary nuclear families with extended family ties to incorporate a sense of community into their everyday life? Part of the answer might be how each uses social networks. Communal utopias tend to have much more extensive social networks and ties. Another reason might be that it is difficult for some nuclear families to suppress nuclear family interests in favor of extended family connections. Maybe we expect too much of both communal groups and nuclear families. Might we be setting them up for failure? As we will see in Chapter 2, certain groups last longer and are more successful because they are more adept at building commitment among their members. Some groups are better able to build commitment among their members because of their organizational structure.

One of the few functions remaining under the family's purview is that of intimacy. In an era of elevated divorce rates, those wishing to learn how to balance the needs of individualism with the demands of community presented by the nuclear family can study the successes and failures of communes regarding the issues of personal autonomy and social order.

Another valid reason for studying cultural alternatives such as communal utopias, is that by investigating the values and social structure of groups that are viewed as radical or who challenge the status quo, one can uncover society's myths and ideologies. As Diane Barthel (1989, p. 242) states,

> I argue that these communes have become symbolic of the possible and the impossible, suggestive of what lies down paths not followed by the rest of the nation. They provide reassurance that, with all of our societal conflicts and contradictions, we are still on the right path.

Communes can teach us much about what it means to be a member of a family, group, or society and how social order is created and sustained. Some communes build their social order on love, others on autonomy and anarchy, still others attempt to control individuals for the good of the community. As Benjamin Zablocki (1980, p. 2) states,

> Most of these experiments fail; the few that succeed are usually drastically modified over time. For the systematic examination of these various ways of trying to modify social structure, communes, their intricate and involuted role sets, and their well-defined but volatile hierarchies, constitute a useful natural laboratory.

Communal utopias are social microcosms and it is useful to learn from their successes and failures. By studying our country's communal past and present, Pitzer (1984a, p. 221) states, we might find some useful information about four key dilemmas, "(1) community versus individuality, (2) cooperation versus competition, (3) authority versus equality, (4) utopia versus dystopia."

The insights of Kanter, Barthel, Zablocki, and Pitzer provide convincing reasons for studying communal utopias. Amitai Etzioni (1996, p. 1) offers another glimpse of how useful the sociological perspective can be in understanding a continuing social paradox—how to balance the concerns of social order while not compromising personal autonomy. Etzioni (1996, p. 1) writes,

> Only a community that is responsive to the "true needs" of all its members, both in the substance of its core/shared values and in its social formation, can minimize the penalties of order and the dangers of autonomy.

Etzioni's concerns can readily be juxtaposed with those of families. Healthy families work to balance social order and personal autonomy, thus allowing an atmosphere where better intimate relationships can develop. Etzioni (1996, p. 3) recommends that the inherent tension between social order and personal autonomy, which we see in our families and communities, can be reduced by making the social order more responsive or amenable to the needs of its members. He acknowledges that this is easier said than done. For example, the Israeli kibbutzim, communal utopias which I will discuss further in Chapter 2, have created responsive communities by balancing the group's social formation with the needs of its individuals and families. Nevertheless, they have not eliminated the tension between these two forces.

Although it is not easy to reduce the tension between these competing forces, Etzioni (1996, p. 10) proposes a tentative solution. He recommends that social processes need to be developed that create "layered loyalties" in the members of different communities. By developing "layered loyalties" members see themselves as belonging to more than one community. The same can be said for communal families. Those communal groups who have developed social processes that link nuclear families to the larger communal family produce stronger social bonds and a sense of community. One of the issues we will discuss is describing those social processes which groups use to build commitment and community.

The concern with developing responsive communities is not a new revelation, but one which has occupied the thoughts of social and moral philosophers for centuries. Sociology began as a discipline during the turbulent times in Europe brought on by three key revolutions, the Protestant Reformation, the French Revolution, and the Industrial Revolution. These revolutions helped to bring down the "old order," and, in the eyes and minds of conservative social philosophers, contributed to the "loss of community." Robert Nisbet (1966, pp. 6-7) identifies community, authority, status, sacred, and alienation as the core ideas around which the study of society emerged. These ideas epitomize traditionalism or the "old order" while society, power, class, secular, and progress are ideas which characterize modernism or the "new order." Communalism is strongly aligned with traditionalism, while individualism is akin to modernism.

The social paradox or probably better put, the social conundrum, which we have been addressing, the issue of social order and personal autonomy, has its roots planted deeply in our psyche and social structure. No one better than Robert Bellah et al. can comment on this phenomenon. Bellah et al. (1985, p. 285) find that our strong sense of individualism undermines our attempts for commitment to one another, and they state,

> What has failed at every level—from the society of nations to the national society to the local community to the family—is integration: we have failed to remember "our community as members of the same body," as John Winthrop put it. We have committed what to the republican founders of our nation was the cardinal sin: we have put our own good, as individuals, as groups, as a nation, ahead of the common good.

Bellah et al. (1985, p. 285) conclude that we are unlikely to seek solutions to our problems because we are ambivalent. We resist social integration because it smacks of utopianism and none of us, or few of us, are willing to venture into attempts to create the perfect society. Our problems have their roots in the Lockean political ideology of individual freedom and individually achieved affluence, while, at the same time, other social institutions such as the economy and government operate in an un-Lockean manner. Bellah et al. (1991, p. 79) believe we have bitten into the illusory apple, while powerful forces work to undermine the common good. By studying those who have ventured into attempts at building community and family, we will hopefully identify and incorporate the best of their outcomes into our social structures and social processes.

Sociology is the study of social processes and social structures. Social processes are patterns of behavior or activity which are the primary means of carrying out social purposes. Social structures are the physical and social arrangements of the members of a group which includes interaction, roles, and statuses. Process refers to the operation of a social structure, the action, activity, or order within an organization. What our concern will be is to discover the means by which communal families structure their social life. By this I mean, we will investigate the norms, values, and processes through which individuals occupy positions in social structures and, for our specific purposes, we will focus on how families, both nuclear and communal family groups, and communal utopias, coexist to produce a shared reality for their members. In particular, we will look at how they conceptualize family, gender roles, work and parental roles, sexual relationships, leadership, and child rearing.

Family and Community

Yaacov Oved (1993, p. 411) aptly describes the dilemma family and communal scholars encounter when they study communal utopias by the following heading he used to begin a chapter on the family and women in communes, "The Family and the Commune: Adverse or Congruous Entities?" Jon Wagner (1986, p. 175) found it is generally agreed upon by scholars that families and communal utopias are theoretically incompatible with one another; communal loyalties compete with familistic loyalties. This was and is the belief of many of the founders of communal utopias and scholars who have assessed these institutions. Kanter (1972, p. 90) found that family ties were potential sources of conflict. The commune was supposed to become the member's new family. She also found, in her study of nineteenth-century communes, that successful communes were more likely than unsuccessful communes to dissolve the nuclear family because they competed for the emotional energy of their members.

The conventional argument about the incompatibility of family and community life is lacking, according to Barry Shenker (1986, p. 219). Exclusive relationships, such as family life, need not necessarily lead individuals away from community life. In fact, Shenker (1986, p. 221) argues that familial relationships can enhance one's satisfaction in the community, which inevitably leads one to be more committed to the goals of the community.

Scholars have inadequately conceptualized this issue because there is still confusion over the nature of communes and the role of the family within communes. In response to the question, "Do communes themselves constitute 'families,' or do communes contain families in their midst?" Kanter (1973, p. 279) concluded that communes are social organizations that can contain families, but usually these families eventually blend in with the community and experience a loss of functions. This is common particularly in larger communes, whereas, she found in hippie and anarchic communes of the 1960s and early 1970s nuclear families were frequently present, although the impression was the commune represented one large communal family group.

The following three theories: a Freudian view exposing the potency of sexual and emotional bonds; a second approach which highlights the role of complete loyalty and devotion of members; and a functionalist approach which challenges the notion that family ties surpass communal ties support Kanter's (1973, p. 280) position that families pose a threat to communal success and longevity.

Communes are also seen as floating back and forth between the ideological images of community and those of family, partly because our social institutions are not equipped to provide the level of intimacy that many communalists seek (Zablocki, 1980, p. 351). Communalists are rather ambivalent about family because they find it difficult to resolve gender and age differences among themselves.

In his discussion of family imagery in communitarian ideology, Zablocki (1980, p. 352) skillfully identifies a key point regarding the role of families in communes. He states,

> But, in this regard, contemporary communes are significantly different from the utopian communities in America during the eighteenth and nineteenth centuries and from the Israeli kibbutzim. The utopias and the kibbutzim strove to develop a familial structure in the hope that this would facilitate the achievement of certain (social, political, and economic) nonfamilial functions. American communes, on the other hand, are looked to by their members for the fulfillment of familial functions without the restrictions of the family structure (e.g., sexual and child-rearing functions without marital and intergenerational responsibilities). The utopias and kibbutzim used family structure to recreate society without impersonality. The communes use voluntaristic structure to recreate family without nuclear dependence.

The interest in communal living and other nontraditional family settings is an attempt to resolve the problems thrust upon families by a changing society (Yinger, 1982, p. 265). Families are now more responsible for being the emotional havens of their residents, while the community at large is withdrawing its support of the family. No wonder the family is viewed as constricting. At the same time, little or no support from the larger community is also distressing.

> What better way to try to resolve the dilemma of feeling both emotionally surrounded and emotionally alone than to join an antifamily family that is at the same time a small community and quasi-family. Some communes and other groups are "antifamily" in the sense of variously opposing such traditional standards as those regarding the place of children, monogamy, and the balance of emphasis on achievement or acceptance. Yet attacks on the family are strongly connected with longing for a family. (Yinger, 1982, p. 266)

Philip Abrams and Andrew McCulloch (1976, p. 125) concur with Yinger's position that possibly communalists are longing for a family. They found that if given a choice between no family at all or a different type of family in which to work out the issues of intimacy and personal autonomy, communalists still chose a family type of setting.

> Communes are not really all that different from ordinary families. The important difference seems to be that unscrambling a "commune" (an introjected set of relations based on recent, conditional choice and a strong sense of equality including sexual equality) is a little easier than unscrambling a "family." (Abrams & McCulloch, 1976, p. 127)

The following set of questions regarding the role of marriage and the family in communal utopias are posed by Jay and Heather Ogilvy (1972, p. 87).

> To the extent that both a marriage and a commune serve the same functions for their members, what kind of context does a commune provide for a marriage? Will the two complement one another, the one making up for the weaknesses of the other, or will the demands of significance compete with one another?

These questions will be answered in the following chapters.

A unique insight from what many would consider a most unusual or startling source is offered by George Hillery (1992, p. 211). From his many years of studying communal organizations, specifically monasteries, Hillery concludes the following.

> Accordingly, from the monastery we learn that it is not the family that is so important to communal organizations but love. And it is not any form of love that is important, but it is agape.

This finding puts the Ogilvy's questions into perspective. Maybe we might be asking the wrong questions about the compatibility of family and commune. Obviously there are other factors at work which influence this aspect of social life. Zablocki (1980, p. 353) concurs with Hillery's finding regarding love. He found that the communitarians he studied valued love. We will discuss Hillery's work further in Chapter 2.

Marriage and family life compete with the group for member commitment, according to E. Burke Rochford (1995, p. 171), thus encroaching on the commune's sphere of influence and control and fostering individualism and familial relationships which detach members from the group. Rochford (1995, p. 172) studied the contemporary Hare Krishna Movement [International Society for Krishna Consciousness (ISKCON)] and found that although ISKCON was no longer able to control the marital and familial dimensions of devotees' lives, the nuclear family had not reduced member commitment to ISKCON as a religious organization, although it had substantially reduced member participation in the collective/communal aspect of ISKCON. In its early years (1960s to 1970s) of development in the United States, ISKCON had a strong communal focus. Further discussion of the Hare Krishna and other alternative religious groups will be continued in Chapter 2.

For the most part communal utopias have exhibited a wide range of arrangements regarding families (Oved, 1993, p. 413). For example, the Shakers practiced celibacy and men and women treated each other as brother and sister, while the Hutterites and the Bruderhof have always integrated nuclear families into the complex of communal life. The vast majority of historical and contemporary communal utopias maintained the monogamous nuclear family and incorporated it into the communal lifestyle in a variety of ways. Examples will be provided throughout this book. Those groups which were more likely to disband the nuclear family were religiously oriented. Groups such as Harmony, Zoar, Ephrata, and the Shakers were attempting to live out what they believed to be key biblical, especially New Testament, tenets. These beliefs elevated the position of celibacy, asceticism, and monasticism. Oved (1993, p. 415) rightly states,

> The rational and emotional motivation that prompted people to join an unfamilistic commune was their religious belief, especially their concept of superiority of spirit over flesh and celibacy over marriage.

After the 1840s, most of the religious communes incorporated nuclear families into the communal structure. One major exception was Oneida, which was founded by John Humphrey Noyes. The Oneidans practiced a phenomenon known as complex marriage, which will be discussed in Chapter 3. The first half of the nineteenth century was a period of intense religious revival and millennial excitement, this explains a good part of the development of religious communes during this era (McLoughlin, 1978).

Whether communes abolished nuclear families or maintained them, they had to design and implement strategies to either compensate for the loss of families or how they were to be incorporated into the communal structure. For those communal utopias that abolished nuclear families, they had to replace all of the functions that those families had provided. This obviously produced some interesting situations for those groups which practiced celibacy. The Shakers compensated for this problem by accepting homeless people (often referred to as "Winter Shakers" because they would appear in late fall and leave in early spring) and orphans. Although the Shakers disbanded nuclear families, they used the family as a metaphor to describe their settlements and referred to each other as brother and sister. In those groups which maintained the family, family functions varied based on the ideology and type of communalism practiced by the group. For example, the Hutterites and Bruderhof have communal dining halls where the main meals are taken, but allow families to have their own apartments (Oved, 1993, p. 417). These issues will be elaborated on in the following chapters.

Andrew Rigby (1974, p. 259) notes that among the major social institutions (religion, family, economy, education, government) many communalists, during the 1960s and early 1970s, felt alienated the most from the nuclear family. They believed that small nuclear families were not capable of fulfilling all of the required social functions of family life and that these functions could be better fulfilled in a larger group. For example, some commune members believed the nuclear family put undue emotional strain on the couple, while communal living provides the opportunity to develop other intimate relationships. These relationships could reduce emotional strain and free people of the restrictiveness of the traditional nuclear family (Rigby, 1974, p. 266).

Others believed that nuclear families oppressed women and were not healthy places to raise children. Rigby (1974, p. 269) found a fair amount of agreement among communalists regarding the negative aspects of the nuclear family.

> The nuclear family system is not the only natural way of organizing social life, and that in its present enclosed and isolated form such a system only serves to separate people from each other rather than promote caring relationships between them. As such it represents a barrier to the attainment of their goal of the family of man.

Only a minority of communes, during the 1960s and 1970s, were concerned with developing families (Aidala, 1983, p. 115). Young adults were more likely to be alienated from all social institutions, not just the nuclear family, and rather than seeking to create alternative families, they were seeking social support for a variety of unconventional beliefs and practices. Angela Aidala (1983, p. 119) cautions scholars and others to not generalize regarding alternative-family communes as being representative of the broader communal movement. This point is well taken. For example, many people assume that illegal drugs and illicit sex were common in modern communes. The truth is rather quite the opposite; yes drugs and sex were a part of communal life for some, especially those who were not members of religious communes, but drugs and sex were not the major reasons for the development of the modern communal movement. It is important for us to remember that the recent communal movement was not a monolithic movement, with the major goal to create a better family form (Aidala, 1983, p. 131).

For many, during the 1960s and 1970s, communal living was both an outcome and an influence of overall family change (Aidala, 1989, p. 311). The family was beginning to experience drastic changes in structure, brought on by a variety of factors including industrialization and urbanization. Communal living was just one of many alternatives people were experimenting with. While many people were shocked by the recent communal movement, the majority of them were unaware that communalism has a lengthy history in the United States and abroad. In addition, Aidala found that former communalists are less likely to have married and are more likely to be living in multi-adult households. Aidala and Zablocki (1991, p. 109) found only 22% of communalists indicated that the reasons they joined a commune were related to family themes. The most common reason given by communalists for joining communes was to develop a "consensual community" (Aidala & Zablocki, 1991, p. 108).

This is an appropriate place to stop and assess the preceding material. While Oved and Wagner are accurate in their assessment that most scholars agree that families and communes are incompatible, I disagree that families and communes are incompatible. I find Shenker's argument that family relationships do not necessarily negatively impinge on community relationships, to be very convincing.

I believe the evidence and discussion which follows, will support my position. I agree with the insights of Kanter, Barthel, Zablocki, and Pitzer regarding the reasons for studying communal utopias. Etzioni's concept (1996) of "layered loyalties" is useful for explaining how communes can develop mutual allegiances between families and the larger group. We will eventually investigate how commitment mechanisms are used by a variety of communal groups to build mutual allegiances.

Bellah and his associates (1991) have put their thumb on the perennial issue of how to reconcile social order and personal autonomy. Communes are works-in-progress which confront this issue on a daily basis. I agree with the work of Yinger, Abrams and McCulloch, Zablocki, and Aidala that concluded while communalists did not specifically set out to create new families, they did gravitate to groups which had family settings. I am also not at all surprised that Rigby and Aidala found a significant number of communalists were critical of the nuclear family, even though they came primarily from loving families. The ethos or mood of the 1960s and 1970s was one which was suspicious of tradition and social institutions.

The primary thesis of this book is that families are an essential component of communal life, unless a reliable substitute is found to replace them and their functions. Can communal family groups replace small nuclear families? I believe the answer to this question is yes, and how this is done will vary based on the ideology of the group and whether or not the nuclear family has been abolished or maintained. Has the controversy among scholars and communalists regarding whether families are destructive to communal living been resolved? I do not think it has, but I hope this book will add to debate as we continue to learn more about how family life and community life are connected to one another. The remaining chapters will attempt to provide answers to these questions.

As we learned earlier, the modern communal movement is not a monolithic movement and the communal movement throughout the last several centuries has not been monolithic in structure. The family has not been a monolith either, although many of us are locked into the image of the traditional nuclear family of mother at home and father as the breadwinner. Family forms are much more pluralistic today. The majority of families in the United States are not classified as traditional nuclear families (Macklin, 1980, p. 175). The following structural characteristics are indicative of nontraditional families: never-married singlehood, nonmarital cohabitation, voluntary childlessness, single-parent, divorce and remarriage, androgynous marriage, extramarital relationships, same-sex intimate relationships, and multi-adult households (Macklin, 1980, p. 176). Communal utopias are one type (multi-adult household) of a growing number of nontraditional families, and it is to that issue that we now direct our attention.

Communes and Nontraditional Families

There are two traditional meanings of family, one that deals primarily with biological relationships and the other which deals with the quality of relationships (Kanter, 1977, p. 77). Kanter sees conventional families moving more and more in the direction of structuring their family relations around the second meaning of family, that is, family as a quality of feeling. Therefore, the family is becoming a place where biological ties are less likely to be the main determinants of intimacy and who constitutes a family member. The postbiological family, as a new family form, allows for greater diversity in composition, form, and meaning. Communes have not orchestrated new family relationships; they have merely highlighted, in a more dramatic and visible way, changes which have been in the making for decades (Kanter, 1979, p. 113). Gilbert Zicklin (1983, p. 9) concurs with Kanter's assessment about these family changes and writes that many in communes lived as couples and raised their own children. What had changed for them was not so much family structure, but the idea of what family life was all about.

Emerging new family forms, such as nontraditional families, are forcing us to critically rethink our definition of family. The traditional nuclear family is being reshaped by communal and noncommunal forces. This is occurring for a variety of reasons, but probably the most notable ones come from the family values debate and what is and is not a family from a public policy point of view. Kanter (1977, p. 77) suggests there is plenty of evidence that indicates family relationships have been shifting for decades to feeling, rather than biological ties. For example, the growth in nontraditional families such as communes, same-sex marriages, reconstituted families due to divorce, single-parent families, nonmarital cohabitation, voluntary childlessness, etc., is a direct result of the changing norms in society regarding family life. Eleanor Macklin (1980, p. 175) defines nontraditional as "all living patterns other than legal, lifelong, sexually exclusive marriage between one man and one woman, with children, where the male is the primary provider and ultimate authority."

Family change is not necessarily seen as something positive, especially the growth in the variety of nontraditional families. The Council on Families in America identifies clear signs of deterioration in the traditional nuclear family brought on by high rates of divorce and high numbers of out-of-wedlock births. Today the council sees less emphasis being put on child-centered families and two-parent families. Family change is equated with family decline (Popenoe, 1993a, p. A48). Felix Berardo (1990, p. 809) concludes that social scientists are finding that new family forms have brought not only more freedom of choice for individuals in their pursuit of fulfillment, but also more problems as well.

There are those who challenge the view that family change is equated with family decline. Mary Jo Bane (1976) and Edward L. Kain (1990) find that the facts about family ties, marriage, and child rearing indicate the family will survive. Families will persist because they provide "stability, continuity, and nonconditional affection." Families are not dying; they are changing as the result of long-term trends connected to the process of industrialization. Stephanie Coontz (1992; 1997), Judith

Stacey (1990), and Arlene Skolnick (1991) write that the family is not in decline and that change should not be equated with decline. Families are not declining, just changing in structure and functions. David Popenoe (1993a, p. A48) summarizes the work of these scholars by saying, "The counterattack urges us to move beyond the 'myth of family decline,' to learn to live with a high divorce rate, and to celebrate 'alternative lifestyles'."

Familism, as a cultural value, has waned and during the last 30 years the American family has declined as an institution (Popenoe, 1993b, p. 528). Popenoe (1993b, p. 535) is particularly concerned with the decline of the traditional nuclear family. Popenoe (1993b, p. 529) defines family in the following way:

> Relatively small domestic group of kin (or people in a kin-like relationship) consisting of at least one adult and one dependent person. This definition is meant to refer particularly to an intergenerational unit that includes (or once included) children, but handicapped and infirm adults, the elderly, and other dependents also qualify. And it is meant to include single-parent families, stepfamilies, nonmarried and homosexual couples, and all other family types in which dependents are involved.

Married couples with no dependents would not be considered a family according to this definition. The key indicator of a family is whether or not there are dependents. It appears from the previous definition, that Popenoe would be supportive of calling certain types of communes families if there are dependents who are being cared for by others in the group.

James Ramey (1978, p. 279) does see the shape of the family changing, but this, he concludes, will not in-and-of-itself lead to the demise of the family. He believes that the nuclear family is a transitional family form and that we are moving toward what he calls "the focal family." Focal families are broadly defined based on the circumstances of the people who inhabit them. Bernard Murnstein (1978) would concur that focal families would facilitate what he sees happening as a movement to intimate lifestyles in alternative nontraditional settings.

Traditional and nontraditional family values and behaviors exist side-by-side in our pluralistic society, according to J. Ross Eshleman (1997, p. 7). He does not want to enter into the debate about whether the family is just changing or declining, but he sees families existing on a continuum varying in form based on the particular values which influence those involved (Eshleman, 1997, p. 8). Eshleman (1997, p. 10) concludes that there are at least three meanings of marriage and the family: first of all it is sacred; second it is a social obligation; and third it is highly personal and individualistic and the use of these meanings will vary based on one's situation and perspective.

Despite all the talk about family change and nontraditional family forms, most Americans still marry, have children, and seek stability and quality in their family life (Rubin, 1983, p. 408). Roger Rubin (1983, p. 408) states, "Only those who remain permanently single and/or never have children will ever really experience a totally alternative lifestyle." He claims that we have always had variations in our family forms and we must be careful not to create new myths about family life to supersede old myths (see Coontz, 1992) about family life.

Communal living is not a new family lifestyle and possibly one reason why there is concern with new family forms is the direction they are taking (Schulterbrandt & Nichols, 1972, p. 430). For example, traditional family forms are more prone to be outwardly directed in their impetus, while new family forms, such as communal families, are more inwardly oriented. Joy Schulterbrandt and Edwin Nichols (1972, p. 432) state, "In one sense, the distinction could be made that in traditional family forms, the drive was to find a mission in life. In the communal family form, the drive is to find a meaning to life."

Herein lies an interesting and illustrative point. Some of those drawn to a communal lifestyle are seekers who have not found what they need and want in more traditional family forms. Seeking quality intimate relationships with more than one other adult could possibly deepen one's understanding of life and therefore, bring more meaning to one's life. The communal environment can enhance one's journey to find meaning and once it is found, the communal structure is no longer needed to sustain the search. For one reason or another, living in community frees one to search and find meaning. Once this occurs, many leave and return to form their own nuclear families (Shey, 1977, p. 613). We know, based on the work of Aidala (1983; 1989), that most communalists were not seeking to form a new family, but for those who did, and for those who were just trying to find themselves, the hypothesis presented by Schulterbrandt and Nichols (1972) appears to be very plausible.

While some join communes because they believe something is missing in their lives, others join because of their interest in sharing resources. Resources include such things as housing, automobiles or other forms of transportation, child care, meal preparation, housework, companionship, etc. The sharing of resources is particularly attractive for single parents and the elderly. Sharing resources is not only an economically sound idea but it is environmentally friendly too.

No matter how you look at it, from whatever perspective, conservative, liberal, or moderate, nontraditional families are "here to stay." As we move into the twenty-first century, the operative word regarding family structure is diversity, not similarity. If we can glean any words of wisdom from the scholars discussed in this section, it is that family life is important to us regardless of what side of the spectrum our politics might be on. Researchers and politicians will continue to debate the definition of family, but in our pluralistic society, we will continue to find various family forms in the future, among them various hybrids of communal families.

Is the communal family movement nothing more than a search for *gemeinschaft* in the modern world? Is it that simple, or is something more complex happening in communal families? Ferdinand Tonnies coined the concept *gemeinschaft,* which means community, to compare and contrast with the concept *gesellschaft,* which means society. These concepts are useful primarily because they describe images of types of social relationships, as well as types of social organizations. These concepts have also been useful for explaining social change, particularly from the traditional world or gemeinschaft to the modern world or gesellschaft. As we discussed in the first section of this chapter, the traditional world was characterized by communal ties where the community came before the individual, whereas in the modern world, the community is no longer at the center of the world; the individual is omnipotent (Nisbet, 1966, p. 78).

According to Nisbet (1966, p. 74),

Gesellschaft acquires its typological importance when we see it as a special type of human relationship: one characterized by a high degree of individualism, impersonality, contractualism, and proceeding from volition or sheer interest rather than from the complex of affective states, habits, and traditions that underlies Gemeinschaft.

The family is the embodiment of gemeinschaft. The three key components of gemeinschaft, "blood, place (land), and mind, or kinship, neighborhood, and friendship," are found in the family (Nisbet, 1966, p. 75). Might we all be drawn in some way to these three components of gemeinschaft, especially since the modern mass society we live in de-emphasizes these factors, primarily for those of us in the middle class?

The five core ideas (community, authority, status, sacred, and alienation), discussed in the first section of this chapter, describe a gemeinschaft world. When the first four ideas are no longer dominant or present the fifth, alienation, is produced. The belief is, one feels alienated when one loses touch with or lacks a connection to, something greater than oneself. Whereas, in the modern or gesellschaft world, the individual is highly valued and instead of being alienated, when not connected with tradition and one's community, one is viewed as having progressed.

Has progress forced some of us to rethink our priorities in life and therefore search for a more traditional or gemeinschaft way of life? John Bennett (1975, p. 20) believes that modern communes are doing just that by attempting to reconnect families and communities by returning to a gemeinschaft philosophy. Maybe past and present communalists know more about what Etzioni (1996) calls "layered loyalties" than we are willing to admit?

Communal utopias are not just attempting to create gemeinschaft environments, they are going beyond that to create familial relations (Bennett, 1975; Kanter, 1972). Zablocki (1980, p. 201) states, "It is argued that communes are alike in their pursuit of some kind of extended or alternative family." Yet, based on research done by Zablocki regarding urban communes, he finds little support for that point of view. Although, the major goal of the urban communes he studied was building consensual communities, he nevertheless concludes, that familial-type relationships might be secondary or latent goals (Zablocki, 1980, p. 202).

In response to the question posed at the beginning of this section, Zablocki (1980, p. 203) provides a concise answer, "Communitarian goals do share at least one important characteristic: the desire for gemeinschaft as an end in itself. The intimacy of relations sought by commune members may or may not reflect a desire for a new family form."

The means to achieve these ends (gemeinschaft) is what appears to be at question among researchers.

It is not surprising that scholars, such as Bennett and Kanter, would come to the conclusions they did regarding communes seeking to develop a new family form, especially since the family is viewed as embodiment of gemeinschaft. Did some communes, both past and modern communes, attempt to develop new family forms? Yes, and this issue will be pursued in the chapters which follow. Zablocki's research provides us with valuable insights on community building. We will discuss in the next chapter his classification of communes, and in Chapter 5, the results of his study.

Conclusion

Part of the discussion in this introductory chapter deals with definitional issues, what Gerry Brudenell (1983, p. 237) sees as our attempt in interpreting the essence of family. We have briefly discussed the issues of social order and personal autonomy and how these impinge on families and communities. We have also investigated a cross section of scholarly opinions regarding the theme of this book, the dilemma of whether families and communes are compatible. We learned that both families and communities are not monoliths. We have encountered the position that maybe the most significant change which has taken place in our society regarding family is not so much the issue of changing family structure, but the changing meaning or essence of family toward feeling rather than biological ties. As Kanter so clearly articulated, families are shifting their focus to improving the quality of family intimacy. For many, their quest for intimacy might bring them to consider nontraditional family forms such as communal utopias.

Preview of Remaining Chapters

The following synopsis highlights the topics which will be covered in the remaining chapters of this book. In Chapter 2, "Communes: Conceptual, Definitional, Theoretical, and Typological Issues," we will delve further into the different types of communes, intentional communities, and communal utopias and their ideologies, as well as their reasons for development, survival, and failure. Rosabeth Moss Kanter's theory of commitment and Benjamin Zablocki's communal typology will provide us with important yardsticks to compare and contrast communal utopias. Although the primary focus of this book is on American communes, we will look at the Israeli Kibbutz for purposes of comparison and because the Kibbutz is an important communal movement and it has an interesting history of dealing with families. We will also investigate monasteries and religious orders; although these are communal groups, they will not be addressed in length in this volume. New Religious Movements, often referred to as cults or nonconventional religions, will be discussed and the connections with communal families will be highlighted. As indicated earlier, we will look at the Hare Krishnas and several other high profile groups.

The Shakers, the Oneida Community, and the Amana Colonies will be studied in Chapter 3, "Families in Historic Communal Utopias: Part 1." A brief historical account of each group will be included, as well as a discussion on such issues as how they conceptualized family, sex and gender roles, work and parental roles, sex relationships, leadership, and child rearing. Kanter's theory of commitment will be applied to several of these groups to see how they developed social processes within their social structures to build commitment and community. Or in other words, we will attempt to identify how these groups institutionalized "layered loyalties."

The Hutterites, one of the most prominent communal groups in the United States and Canada, will be featured in Chapter 4, "Families in Historic Communal Utopias: Part 2." The Hutterites arrived in the United States in the latter part of the nineteenth century and their population continues to grow necessitating the creation of new colonies on an almost annual basis. Besides the Hutterites, Chapter 4 will investigate family life among the Ephrata Cloister, Rappites, Zoarites, Mormons, Icarians, Fourierists, Owenites, and Janssonists.

Studies by Benjamin Zablocki, Rosabeth Moss Kanter, and Noreen Cornfield (1983) and others will be used in Chapter 5, "Urban and Rural Communes of the 1960s and 1970s," to examine who joined these communes and the reasons why they wanted to live communally. The attitudes communalists had toward marriage, the family, and communal living will be addressed. Both religious and secular communes will be included.

Data gathered in a rural California commune will be used to create a portrait of communal families and how a post-hippie "family" commune dealt with such issues as child rearing and intimacy. Data from a study of thirteen rural communes will be assessed by looking at how these groups utilized commitment mechanisms. Several other studies will also be consulted to broaden the presentation on rural communes.

A study, conducted by the author in Chicago, of urban religious communes will be used as the basis of discussion in Chapter 6, "Urban and Rural Communes of the 1980s and 1990s." Data from the *Communities Directory: A Guide to Cooperative Living* will be used to create a profile of family life in intentional communities in the 1980s and 1990s. Jesus People USA of Chicago, a contemporary urban religious commune, and Twin Oaks of Louisa, Virginia, a contemporary secular rural commune, will be highlighted as examples of successful communes that have endured for over 20 years.

The major points of this book will be summarized in Chapter 7, "What Have We Learned About Families and Communes?" This chapter will review the arguments and questions put forth earlier in previous chapters. The future of communal living and communal families will be assessed in light of the data and theories discussed by the author.

This book is different in many respects from those which have preceded it on this topic. First of all, the topic, communal families, is usually addressed as a chapter in a book or as a section of a chapter. We are devoting a whole book to communal families. Second, most books dealing with the communal movement and/or nontraditional families are narrow in scope. What I mean by this is that they look only at a particular type of commune or nontraditional family. For example, a book on contemporary communes often excludes a thorough discussion on historic communes, and a book on historic communes often excludes commentary on contemporary communes. We will look at both of these time frames. Third, this book will bring together, under one cover, a discussion of two of the most interesting social ideas, family and community.

2

Communes

Conceptual, Definitional, Theoretical, and Typological Issues

This chapter will continue to introduce the reader to the scholarly literature on communal groups. The purpose of this chapter is not to provide an exhaustive review of the literature on communal living, for that would be beyond the scope of this book, and a massive undertaking in its own right. What is relevant for this study is to discuss some of the key conceptual, definitional, theoretical, and typological issues related to the study of communes and our topic of communal families. In order to understand communal families, one needs to know some elementary background information on communes. Much of this chapter will be based on some recent work I have done on the communal movement (Smith, 1996a).

Conceptual and Definitional Issues

There are as many definitions of communal living as there are scholars studying this phenomenon. There are no generic or agreed upon definitions. Definitions of concepts tend to be study specific, varying from researcher to researcher, but there is the tendency to use some concepts interchangeably as I have done with communes, communal utopias, and intentional communities.

Lyman T. Sargent (1994) struggled with this definitional dilemma while trying to find a term which was inclusive enough to describe the variety of communal living situations to be found in modern society. Sargent (1994, p. 13) identified 19 concepts that are used with some regularity by scholars to describe communal living: "intentional community, intentional society, communal society, cooperative community, practical utopia, commune, withdrawn community, enacted community, experimental community, communal experiment, alternative lifestyle, communitarian experiment, socialist colonies, collective settlement, mutualistic communities, communistic societies, utopian society, and utopian experiment."

This listing is not exhaustive; there are many other terms used to describe communal living such as alternative communities and, a term I have used frequently, communal utopias, which have not been included in this list.

Intentional community is the most representative concept of what Sargent (1994, p. 15) envisioned communal living to be and he defined it as "a group of five or more adults and their children, if any, who come from more than one nuclear family and who have chosen to live together to enhance their shared values or for some other mutually agreed upon purpose."

The Fellowship for Intentional Community, publishers of the *Communities Directory: A Guide to Cooperative Living*, also supports the use of intentional community as a universal term to describe communal living, but they struggle, as well, to create an even more inclusive definition of intentional community. They began using the term intentional community back in the early 1950s when the former organization, Fellowship of Intentional Communities, discarded the term cooperative community.

Twin Oaks, a secular, rural commune in Virginia, which we will study in Chapter 6, has the following belief about the meaning of intentional community, according to Kinkade (1994, p. 1),

> The essential element in any intentional community, ours included, is that people who want to live in it have to join, be accepted by those who already live there, and go by its rules and norms, which may in some ways differ from those in society at large.

While Zablocki's (1980, p. 7) definition of communal living is similar to Sargent's, he prefers to use the term commune rather than intentional community. Zablocki believes a commune is created "for an indefinite period of time" and focuses on "achievement of community."

Some scholars, including Timothy Miller (1990, p. xxvii), find it easier to recognize intentional community than define it. A commune, for Miller, has three components: geographical proximity, economic sharing, and a common vision.

The use of intentional community, as an inclusive term, to represent communal living is a viable option. The same can be said for communal utopias, which was defined in Chapter 1. Commune continues to be used today, but in certain circles its meaning carries a negative connotation. This negativity stems from the publicity several of the more avant-garde communes received regarding illegal drug use and illicit sex. Images live on long past their time, even more so when they are not completely accurate.

Various attempts by researchers have been made to clarify the conceptual and definitional dilemma by differentiating between three concepts: commune, intentional community, and collective. Communes consist of five or more adults, who share housing, meals, finances, labor, and a common purse. Intentional communities are less encompassing than communes; they share some resources and pool finances on a less systematic basis. Collectives are communal arrangements which share living expenses. The major difference between these three types of arrangements is that as one moves from commune to intentional community to collective the less likely there is a specific ideology and/or lifestyle that links the members to one another. The group is likely to become more inclusive and less idealistic as one moves from commune to collective (Conover, 1978, p. 5).

Communes, collectives, cooperatives, intentional communities, and experimental communities have also been defined as consisting of three or more adults who are linked to one another by some form of sharing. Richard Fairfield (1972, p. 1) found communes are the most radical form of communitarianism where members share housing, income, expenses, meals, child rearing, and even sex. Collectives are less radical than communes; they do not share as much but they do share more with each other than do cooperatives. Cooperatives are the most conservative type of communitarian group because they own their individual homes and have independent jobs. Intentional communities tend to be planned, while experimental communities are the most flexible of the five groups.

Again, what differentiates these groups from one another is the degree of sharing between members.

Up until now, we have focused on a selection of the various terms and definitions used in the literature for communal living. In Chapter 1, I provided a brief definition of utopia. Now, I will elaborate further on that concept and its connection with communitarianism.

Utopia is often used in a pejorative sense, according to William McCord (1989, p. 17) and is perceived of as a place of perfection, something beyond human attainment. Sargent (1994, p. 3) acknowledges that utopia can be both a positive and/or a negative place, while for Ruth Levitas (1990, p. 8) utopia is best seen as a desire for a better way of life.

Utopias can be classified into three types: exhorted, imposed, and communitarian. For our purposes, we will focus only on communitarian utopias because the majority of utopian undertakings have been communitarian in design. We encounter a similar dilemma with discussing utopias as we do with types of communal living. Another complication, as well, is the controversy among scholars as to whether or not communal societies are utopian (Zablocki, 1980, p. 7).

Communes are different from other communitarian utopias and Ron Roberts (1971, p. 10) considers them a subclass of utopias. He found that modern communes generally reject hierarchy and social status, bureaucracy, and are relatively small in size. These are traits which are opposite of what one would have found among the majority of traditional communitarian utopias. Although, it needs to be noted, there are modern communitarian utopias that also reject these three traits.

In response to the question of whether or not communal societies are utopian, Pitzer (1984a, p. 240) concludes that many of them are and states, "If only briefly, in these intentional communities, and possibly in these communities alone, humanity has realized relations and institutions that have made utopia 'now here' rather than 'no where'."

There is a connection between utopianism and communitarianism, according to Sargent (1994, p. 13), and groups based on B. F. Skinner's book *Walden Two,* such as Twin Oaks of Louisa, Virginia, who have incorporated utopian ideas into their design and everyday life, are examples of utopian and communitarian groups. While Sargent sees a link between utopianism and communitarianism, Abrams and McCulloch (1976, p. 35) disagree and argue that communes are not pure utopian communities. Kanter (1972, p. 216) also questions whether communes incorporate a utopian ideology into their daily life. Both Abrams and McCulloch (1976) and Kanter (1972) acknowledge the major difference between communes and utopian communities is that in utopian communities the individual is second to the community, whereas in modern communes, individual needs appear to supersede group needs. Kanter (1972, p. 5) sees communes sharing some of the utopian ideals that characterized earlier groups, but most either form anarchistic groups, who retreat from and reject society, or intentional groups, who create a community around a shared set of values. Kanter is correct when she concludes that communes dissolve because they have not incorporated the order that is part of a utopian ideology.

I prefer to use the terms communes, communal utopias, and intentional communities to describe communal living arrangements. As readers will notice, I use these terms interchangeably. I agree with Pitzer's conclusion that many communes are utopian in nature, even if only for a "shining moment," but I find the previous argument by Abrams, McCulloch, and Kanter, regarding the major differences between communes and utopian communities, is equally as compelling.

Historical Trends in North America

Now that we have some background regarding the conceptual and definitional issues in the study of communes, let us turn to a discussion focusing on the trends in communal living. It is difficult to pinpoint exactly how many people have lived communally or are living communally. It is equally difficult to calculate the number of intentional communities, past and present. As you can imagine, based on our previous discussion, how one defines communal living will impact the number of communal utopias and communalists there are. Also, many communes and their members, for a variety of reasons, choose to remain anonymous and uncounted. The best we can do is estimate and our estimations and projections are subject to error, as is all measurement.

The most comprehensive listing of communal utopias compiled to date can be found in a new book edited by Pitzer (1997a, pp. 449-494). This is a list of American communal utopias established by 1965. One

of the most fertile periods of communal growth in the United States has
been omitted from this listing, the period from 1965 to 1975.

One of the most cited directories of communal groups has been compiled by Oto Okugawa (1980). He identified 270 communal and utopian settlements in existence at one time or another from 1787 to 1919.
Of these groups, 141 were functioning sometime during 1860 to 1914
(Fogarty, 1990). Oved (1993, p. viii) found 277 utopias during the years
from 1663 to the 1930s. Kanter (1972) identified 124 communal utopias that were in existence at sometime between 1780 and 1860.

As with historic intentional communities, the number of modern
communes fluctuates depending on the source. Patrick Conover (1978)
estimated, excluding traditional religious communes such as monasteries, that there were at least 3,000 communal utopias present during 1971
to 1974 and 30,000 to 40,000 men, women, and children inhabited
these communes. Fairfield (1972) calculated there were over 2,000 communes and at least several thousand urban cooperatives and collectives
in 1969 to 1970.

One must keep in mind that scholars generally agree that the modern
communal movement peaked in the late 1960s and early 1970s. It was
both a rural and an urban phenomenon concentrated primarily, but not
exclusively, along the coastal areas of the nation.

Judson Jerome (1974) estimated that 750,000 people lived communally during the 1960s, which was 3% of the population at the time.
Zicklin (1983) calculated that one tenth of 1% of the population was
living communally during the 1960s and 1970s. Ruth Cavan (1976)
identified 512 groups functioning in 1975 and noted that 134 other
groups had disbanded during the previous 3 years. Hugh Gardner
(1978) found at least 600 communal utopias had been in existence by
1965, and only a mere 30% lasted longer than 5 years. Zablocki (1980)
identified at least 1,000 rural communes by 1970 and estimated that 2%
of the population was living communally in 1980. Marguerite Bouvard
(1975) discovered at least 500 communes and collectives in Vermont
alone during the 1960s.

As one can see, the estimates on the number of groups and members
living communally, in the 1960s and 1970s, vary depending on the
source. Miller (1992a; 1995) has identified 100 hippie communes from
the 1960s that still survive in the 1990s. He concludes that there were

probably thousands of communes during the 1960s and 1970s with tens or hundreds of thousands of members.

Communal living has been in a state of decline since 1975, according to Zablocki (1980, p. 357), but there were isolated successful communes which survived and eventually communal living would become popular again. Based on the next set of figures, it appears communal living is still a viable alternative lifestyle.

There were 186 alternative communities in 1990, with 8,000 adults and 2,000 children residing within them (Questenberry & Rock, 1995). Brian Berry (1992) used the 1991 *Communities Directory: A Guide to Cooperative Living* to identify 359 North American communes. Of these communes, 120 were started in the middle to late 1980s and only 20 were founded before 1960. Another 120 were founded in 1965 to 1975 and an additional 50 were just beginning in 1991. An additional 75 communes were identified but decided not to be included in the *Communities Directory*. Most of these new groups are small; only 58 of the 359 communal utopias have more than 50 members. Of these communes, 25% are religiously oriented and 75% are secular in ideology.

As of the mid-1990s, researchers estimated there to be between 3,000 and 4,000 communes (D. Pitzer, personal communication, January 16, 1998). We have information on 400 of them. Based on the 1995 edition of the *Communities Directory: A Guide to Cooperative Living,* there are 50 new communities which were started in the early 1990s. More than 160 have been in existence for at least a decade and 80 others for more than two decades.

Needless to say, even though the numbers vary widely, it is obvious that many people are choosing to live this lifestyle. There have been a variety of rationales offered by scholars to explain the reasons for the development of communal utopias. The scholars in the following section are those most widely respected for their theories on the development of communitarianism.

The Development of Communitarianism

Communal development in the United States has been concentrated into four periods commencing with 1842 to 1848, 1894 to 1900, the

1930s, and the 1960s (Barkun, 1984, p. 36). These periods, or what are often referred to as waves of development, coincided with periods of millennial anticipation. An interesting and often overlooked point is that the majority of historic communal utopias were started by progressive or postmillenarians. These groups believed that Christ's second appearance had already happened. Michael Barkun's (1984, p. 43) most significant contribution to the debate about the reasons for communal development, is that communal development occurs in 50- to 55-year waves or Kondratiev waves. These are periods of accelerations and decelerations of prices and markets. An example would be deflationary depressions.

Utopian development is linked to millenarian impulses which are started by long-wave crises or economic fluctuations (Berry, 1992, p. xv). Economic, religious, and political events are linked to communal and utopian development. Brian Berry believes capitalism and utopian development are connected and argues that utopian expansion in the 1790s, 1820s, 1840s, 1870s, and 1890s was directly correlated with long-wave crises. Long-wave crises are connected with capitalist crises which occur at regular intervals; these crises encouraged progressive millenarians to start utopian settlements.

Religion, economics, and politics affect utopian development. McLoughlin (1978, p. 8) sees ecological, psychological, and other social factors influencing this development and identifies five great awakenings or periods of ideological transformation in the United States: the Puritan Awakening, the period preceding the revolutionary war, the period after the writing of the Constitution, the period after the Civil War, and the most recent period beginning in 1960.

The following five factors spurred utopian development: a frontier with land for the taking, a tradition of independent communities, a belief that perfection was attainable in this new land, liberty and religious freedom, and plenty of immigrants seeking a new and better life in America. These factors, coupled with the strong beliefs and practices of committed groups of radical dissenting European Protestants, fostered the development of communal utopias in the United States (Oved, 1993, p. 3).

Three key themes, according to Kanter (1972, p. 8), are linked with three distinct waves of communitarian development. Religious issues influenced the development of many communes up through 1845, while economic and political issues influenced groups in the 1820s continuing through the 1930s, peaking in the 1840s. The third period is referred to as the psychosocial period and this began after World War II peaking in the late 1960s and early 1970s. This last period was supposedly a reaction to the alienation and isolation experienced by a growing segment of young people, thus promoting the seeking of personal growth among individuals within a communal or more gemeinschaft, traditional environment. Religious, economic, political, and psychosocial issues were not just time specific factors. These factors have had widespread influence up through the present time.

These scholars have pinpointed several key processes which have influenced the development of not just utopian communities, but also the United States as a whole. Religious, political, economic, psychological, and other social factors have over time shaped the fabric of society, our norms, values, and social structure. The influence of these processes have fluctuated based on the historical period and the interaction which occurs between these processes. History is important to know for a variety of reasons, none more important than the fact that history repeats itself and we can learn from it.

Now that we have talked about some conceptual and definitional issues, as well as some of the trends in communal living (see Table 2.1) and the reasons for its development, we will turn our attention to a presentation on theoretical issues, communal types, and ideologies. Even the best typologies miss important ideas. Typologies, by their vary nature, are designed to be inclusive, which can lead to overlap and the lack of mutual exclusivity. While this might be a potential problem, typologies are useful and necessary heuristic tools.

As we will see, not all communes are alike, just as not all families are alike. Communal goals and structures vary with the ideology of the individual groups and as we will see so do the use of commitment mechanisms which, according to Kanter (1972), will help determine longevity and success in organizations.

Theoretical Issues

Kanter (1972) developed a theory of commitment to explain why certain organizations fail and others succeed. She was concerned with

TABLE 2.1 The Number of Communal Utopias

Historic Communal Utopias		
Source	Number	Time Frame
Oved (1993)	277	1663-1930s
Okugawa (1980)	270	1787-1919
Kanter (1972)	124	1780-1860
Fogarty (1990)	141	1860-1914
Modern Communal Utopias		
Source	Number	Time Frame
Conover (1978)	3,000	1971-1974
Fairfield (1972)	2,000	1969-1970
Cavan (1976)	512	1975
Gardner (1978)	600	1965
Zablocki (1980)	1,000	1970
Pitzer (1998)	4,000	1998

how groups exert control over their members and she wanted to identify what processes groups used to enhance commitment. Kanter found that those nineteenth-century communal groups that incorporated as many of the following commitment mechanisms as possible were more likely to survive and be successful. These mechanisms build commitment in three significant areas: commitment to the organization, commitment to the members, and commitment to the ideas of the community. Correspondingly, these types of commitment are referred to as instrumental commitment, affective commitment, and moral commitment. A deficiency in any of these areas can contribute to the weakening of ties that bind people to groups and organizations, and in our case to communal groups, reducing a group's chances for longevity and success.

There are six mechanisms, two for each type of commitment. Sacrifice and investment are processes which enhance instrumental commitment and the continuance of the commune. Renunciation and communion are processes which enhance affective commitment and contribute to the development of cohesion within the community. Mortification

TABLE 2.2 Kanter's Commitment Mechanisms

1. Sacrifice	Something is given up as a condition or price of membership either through abstaining from something and/or shunning comfort and living austerely.
2. Investment	Members invest their labor, time, and financial resources in the community therefore creating a stake in the community. They are less likely to leave the community if they are not compensated in some way for these items.
3. Renunciation	Relationships outside the group are relinquished to insure that members are emotionally committed only to the new group. Family, couple, and parental relationships are often altered or terminated.
4. Communion	A strong sense of unity with the group is created through communal sharing, homogeneity, communal labor, regularized group contact, ritual, and possibly even some type of persecution experience.
5. Mortification	A new identity is formed for the individual by his affiliation with others in the group. This is accomplished through confession and mutual criticism, sanctions, spiritual differentiation, and deindividualization.
6. Transcendence	The group becomes the center of power, meaning, and significance. This is achieved by groups and leaders who inspire through ideology, power, and authority as well as through guidance, ideological conversion, and tradition.

SOURCE: Adapted from Kanter, 1972.

and transcendence are processes which enhance moral commitment and enable the community to have more control over its members. The instrumental, affective, and moral or evaluative mechanisms help to link the personality system with the social system of the group thus contributing to continuance, cohesion, and control.

Sacrifice, renunciation, and mortification are detaching mechanisms. They help to sever the ties and connections members have outside of the community. Investment, communion, and transcendence are attaching mechanisms. What detaching mechanisms erase attaching mechanisms replace. They do this by binding the member to commune and strengthening his or her relationship with their new group. Sacrifice

might involve relinquishing something as a requirement for membership, while investment might involve contributing resources to the
group. Renunciation might involve terminating relationships with those
outside of the group, while communion builds commitment by empha-
sizing shared characteristics. Mortification involves building a new identity based on group membership, while transcendence involves buying
into the ideology of the group. Table 2.2 presents a summary of Kanter's
commitment mechanisms. These mechanisms will be used to help explain the structural arrangements and organizational strategies of some
of the historic and modern communes we will begin investigating in
Chapter 3.

Nineteenth-century communes used all of the mechanisms, but the
transcendence and communion mechanisms were used the most followed by sacrifice, renunciation, investment, and mortification (Kanter,
1972). Gardner (1978) looked at modern rural communes in the 1960s
and 1970s and concluded that these groups used fewer commitment
mechanisms than the nineteenth-century communes. Investment, renunciation, and mortification were found to be strongly related to communal survival, while sacrifice, communion, and transcendence were
weakly related to survival.

I studied urban religious communes in the early 1980s and found that
communion, mortification, and transcendence were used at moderate
or higher levels, while sacrifice, investment, and renunciation were not
widely used (Smith, 1984; 1986). Based on Kanter's, Gardner's, and my,
studies we see quite a variation in the use of these mechanisms. Part of
the explanation for this variation is provided by some interesting work
done by John Hall (1988).

Not all groups have the capabilities to use commitment mechanisms
in similar ways (Hall, 1988, p. 679). A group's cultural pattern of social
organization determines whether or not they have the capacity to use
commitment mechanisms. Certain communal utopias, because of the
influence cultural structures have on the relationship between the individual and the group, such as worldly utopian communities and other-
worldly sects (to be discussed later), are successful due to their social
organization. Differing assumptions about human nature and social life
lead to the construction of different value systems and structural arrangements by communes (Niv, 1980, p. 379).

Four commitment factors explain almost 70% of the variance in group success. Ethnicity and homogeneity enhance affective commitment thus producing cohesion, while confession and spiritual hierarchy enhance moral commitment or social control. Success in worldly utopian communities is dependent on a strong sense of communion which is reinforced through ethnicity and homogeneity, while other-worldly sects rely on developing a strong sense of mortification which is influenced by confession and spiritual hierarchy which is tied to transcendence (Hall, 1978).

Kanter's (1972) theory is one useful explanation for the success and failure of communal utopias. Sacrifice, renunciation, and mortification modify the role of individualism, while investment, communion, and transcendence contribute to maintaining a sense of social order. Social order and personal autonomy are influenced then by the use of commitment mechanisms. These mechanisms can also be considered as the social processes that build "layered loyalties" between members and the community (Etzioni, 1996).

While success can be measured by longevity and the use of commitment mechanisms, an emerging theory, developmental communalism, postulates that those groups that imposed inflexible membership requirements, such as a lifetime commitment to community of goods, contributed to the eventual downfall of community life. Whether a group is successful or not depends not so much on longevity, but rather on did the community fulfill its goals (Pitzer, 1997a). Pitzer (1989, p. 70) argues that,

> We can begin putting the terms "success" and "failure" to better use, if we choose to use them at all. Success and failure can be used to measure the extent to which original and long-range goals are achieved and people inside and outside movements are benefited rather than to suggest how long a communal framework is maintained.

Now that we have been introduced to Kanter's theory, which helps us understand how communities use structural arrangements and organizational strategies to promote and sustain commitment and the life of the community, let us turn to a discussion of communal typologies or ways of categorizing different communal utopias. Kanter's theory can be applied to any group or organization, not just communes.

TABLE 2.3   Hall's Typology of Utopian Communal Groups

	Mode of Organizing Time		
	Diachronic	*Synchronic*	*Apocalyptic*
Mode of Social Enactment			
Natural		Commune	
Produced	Worldly utopian international association	Worldly utopian community	Sects: warring/ other-worldly
Transcendental		Ecstatic association	

SOURCE: Adapted from Hall, J. R. (1978). *The Ways Out: Utopian Groups in an Age of Babylon* (p. 202). London: Routledge and Kegan Paul. Used with permission.

Typological Issues

Table 2.3 contains a typology of communal groups which includes five ideal types (Hall, 1978, p. 202). Hall argues that communal groups differ from one another according to two phenomenological dimensions: their understanding of time and their mode of social enactment or how they construct their social reality. He relied on the work done previously by Karl Mannheim (1936) on utopian thought and the use of time. Three modes of organizing time are diachronic, synchronic, and apocalyptic (Hall, 1987, p. 11). Diachronic time deals with a linear succession of moments, while synchronic time focuses on the moment not on a continuous linear succession of time. Apocalyptic time emphasizes the end of historical time, the last days of life as we know it.

The three modes of social enactment are natural, produced, and transcendental. The experiences one has in a natural mode are viewed as real and valid. The experiences one has in a produced mode tend to be coherent, unified, and create a comprehensive system of belief. A transcendental mode of social enactment is one where reality is created and sustained through meditation and religious insight (Hall, 1978, p. 12).

The following communal groups are created by combining a specific mode of organizing time, with a specific mode of social enactment: commune, worldly utopian intentional association, worldly utopian community, sects—warring/other-worldly, and ecstatic association. The commune is a natural synchronic type, the worldly utopian intentional association is a produced diachronic type, the worldly utopian community is a produced synchronic type, the warring sect is a produced apocalyptic type, and the other-worldly sect is a produced apocalyptic type, and the ecstatic association is a transcendental synchronic type (Hall, 1978, p. 202).

Communes tend to be pluralistic and eclectic, while intentional associations are rational and bureaucratic. Utopian communities rely very strongly on communion mechanisms to meet their goals, while apocalyptic warring sects are charismatic communities and apocalyptic other-worldly sects withdraw from society and focus on the sacred. Ecstatic associations use meditation to help them construct a reality which is above the mundane aspects of everyday life.

A much less complicated typology was developed by Miller (1990, p. xx), who found the most efficient way to classify communes was to identify them as either religious or secular, which he did for the time period from 1860 to 1960. He created ten sets of religious communes (Anabaptists, other committed-conservative Protestants, Jews, Mormons, Theosophists, Adventists, the egalitarians and liberationists, other Protestant social reformist communities, Oriental groups, and a heading for all the remaining) and nine sets of secular communities (socialist communes, anarchist communities, the single tax enclaves, the Fellowship of Intentional Communities groups, ethnic communities, special-purpose communities, the last gasp of Fourierism, back to the land/opening of the West, and the secular visionaries and utopians). Many of these groups continue to thrive today. These nineteen groupings contain many other subgroupings within each category, therefore unlimited typologies could be created to distinguish between communes.

Abrams and McCulloch (1976, p. 38) identify four types of communes: the quasi-commune, the utopian community, the purposive community, and the family commune. They found that only about half of the communes they studied were truly communes, according to their definition, "Groups devoted to communal living for its own sake as a way of institutionalizing friendship within and around a chosen domestic place" (Abrams & McCulloch, 1976, p. 33).

The most complete commune, and the least studied and understood, is the secular family commune, and Abrams and McCulloch (1976,

p. 38) focused on this type in their study of British communes. They state that secular family communes are the most complete because they encompass what is essential.

> There is a sense of group identity, that members want to be the best of friends and that the group is expected to function as a household and a family; but also that it is expected to function as a world in the sense that the majority of each member's social interaction, or at least that part of it which is felt to be deeply important, takes place within the group. (Abrams & McCulloch, 1976)

Although our focus is on American communes, we will return to this study in Chapter 4 and review Abram and McCulloch's findings on British family communes for purposes of comparison.

George Melynk (1985, p. 9) distinguished between four types of cooperative forms: liberal democratic, Marxist, socialist, and communalist. The communalist tradition or emphasis has both religious and political branches and this tradition is characterized by four features: isolation, charismatic leadership, small intimate community, and egalitarianism. Although these features appear to be repeated across the communal landscape, Melynk (1985, p. 79) concludes that communes do not always relate well.

> There is little perceived commonality by the members of a Hutterite colony, of a monastery, or of a countercultural commune. Since their beliefs are different, even when their practice is similar, their common communal lifestyle is insufficient to overcome differences. Communes that survive do so by clinging tenaciously to their own particular ideology.

The previous quote is appropriate and a good reminder that not all communes are alike, and just because some one lives communally does not necessarily mean they have had the same experiences or see and experience reality in a similar way as another communalist from another commune. Communal researchers attempt to reconstruct the reality experienced and lived by communalists. Essentially, much of social science is about reconstructing reality and these typologies help us to understand these social worlds. Keep in mind, these classifications are ideal types meaning they are approximations of what researchers think they have found or others will find. They are not found in their pure form. One

TABLE 2.4 Zablocki's Eight Types of Commune Ideologies

	Strategic Philosophy		
Locus of Attention	Consciousness	Direct Action	
Spiritual World	Eastern	Christian	Religious Communes
Individual Self	Psychological	Rehabilitational	
Primary Group Community	Cooperative	Alternative Family	Secular Communes
Secular Society	Countercultural	Political	

SOURCE: Reprinted with the permission of The Free Press, a Division of Simon & Schuster. From *Alienation and Charisma: A Study of Contemporary American Communes*, by Benjamin Zablocki. ©1980 by The Free Press.

of the most useful typologies of communal groups was developed by Zablocki (1980) based on his study of rural and urban communes of the 1960s and 1970s.

Table 2.4 identifies eight types of commune ideologies (Zablocki, 1980, p. 204). Commune types were determined by their strategic philosophy and locus of attention. Strategic philosophy included either a strategy of consciousness (or non-action) or a strategy of direct action. These were the two most important strategic philosophies in the communitarian thinking of that time. Locus of attention was divided into four categories: spiritual world, individual self, primary group community, and secular society. These loci of attention were the major concerns of communalists.

The consciousness ideologies were Eastern, psychological, cooperative, and countercultural groups, while the direct action ideologies were Christian, rehabilitational, alternative-family, and political groups. The Eastern and Christian groups were religious communal utopias focusing on the spiritual world. Psychological and rehabilitational groups were secular communes focusing on the individual self. Cooperative and alternative-family groups were also secular communes whose focus was developing primary group community, while countercultural and political groups were secular communes as well and their focus was secular society. The most significant differences regarding social structure and membership occurred between the religious and secular intentional communities, rather than between the consciousness and direct action groups (Zablocki, 1980, p. 205).

Eastern communes included Hindu, Buddhist, Sikh, or homegrown varieties, while Christian communes were distinguished as evangelical youth, charismatic renewal, sectarian withdrawal, and social gospel. Psychological communes focused on self-actualization and were labeled as either mystical, gestalt, or psychosexual. Rehabilitational communes were primarily concerned with helping people heal damaged and weak identities. Cooperative communes attempted to create a collective living situation and were identified as either cooperative households, cooperative enterprises, "crash pad" communes, or devolved utopias. Alternative-family groups worked at establishing new family structures and forms not based on blood ties. They believed the nuclear family was obsolete and were classified as patriarchal, fraternal, matriarchal, or group marriage. Countercultural communes were populated primarily by hippies and consisted of cultural demonstration projects, hippie farms or houses, tribal settlements, or utopian reservations. Political communes were imbued by the beliefs of the New Left and those who were moving in the direction of anarchism and socialism. Political communes were labeled as socialist, anarchist, or social democratic (Zablocki, 1980).

Of the eight commune types, the one of most interest to us is the alternative-family. Since one of the major themes of this book is to investigate communal families, a brief comment on what Zablocki found is pertinent. Of the 60 rural and 60 urban communes, he studied only 11 of them, 6 rural and 5 urban, that were alternative-family communes. Of the 11 studied, 2 were patriarchal, 2 matriarchal, 6 fraternal (where the emphasis is on equality and adults treat each other as brothers and sisters), and 1 group marriage. Alternative-family communes tend to be isolated and they are more stable, sophisticated, and middle class than other types. They value long-term commitment to the development of an extended family, but they rarely achieve it (Zablocki, 1980, p. 243). We will return to this study in Chapter 4 to review his specific findings of alternative-families, as well as families which were present in some of the other communal types of the 1960s and 1970s.

There are other typologies that have been developed by researchers to catalog communal groups, but I believe the ones we discussed are the most useful, as well as the most representative, of the typologies. These typologies, especially Zablocki's and Hall's, were geared to explaining the modern communal movement. One last typology can assist us in summarizing this section and providing a connection between modern and historic communal groups.

Two additional types are retreat and service communes (Kanter, 1972, p. 174). Retreat communes, in most cases, lack a shared ideology or in other words are "noncreedal." They are unintentional communities formed more by happenstance and for convenience and are typically anarchistic in character. Retreat communes have very permeable boundaries. Boundary maintenance is an important social process or activity for any group which is interested in surviving. Groups with more permeable boundaries tend to use fewer commitment mechanisms. Service communes are ideology based or "creedal" and more similar to the utopias of the past. Service communes are intentional communities created with specific goals in mind. They tend to have very strong boundaries which contribute to the group's ability to build a strong communal identity.

Although I find explanatory value in all of these typologies, Zablocki's typology is extremely useful for explaining the variation among the various communal living settings. Reflect back a moment to the beginning of this chapter, where we discussed the various terms used to describe communal living settings. Sargent, Conover, and Fairfield identified a variety of types of communal living situations including, communes, cooperatives, and collectives. Zablocki's typology incorporates these different communal arrangements and differentiates between them. It is not a cumbersome model and it clearly delineates the locus of attention and the strategic philosophy of the eight categories of communes.

Cults, Monasteries, and Kibbutzim

Before moving onto the next chapter, we need to reflect a bit more about communal types. As we learned earlier, Zablocki's (1980, p. 205) typology separates communes into two major groups, religious and secular. Religious communes are divided into two categories, Eastern and Christian. Within each of these we will find religious cults. Communes are often mistaken for cults and vice versa. Cults are one type of religious organization. Sociologically speaking, cults are the beginning stage of new religions.

Many people find it surprising that Christianity began as a cult and that Jesus Christ was a cult leader. They find this intriguing because of the current nonscientific usage of the term cult. Some other cult leaders you might have heard of are Bhagwan Shree Rajneesh, Jim Jones, David Koresh, Sun Myung Moon, and Swami Prabhupada. Can some communes be classified as cults? Yes, most certainly, and we will be looking at religious communes in the following chapters. Unfortunately, the term cult is used in a pejorative sense by the media and the anticult movement. Its meaning has come to reflect a dangerous group, where people are coerced and frequently brainwashed. This is unfair and biases how the public and even how some scholars, who should know better, view religious communes. Some scholars prefer to refer to cults as new religious movements (NRMs) or nonconventional or alternative religions, to avoid the popular meaning attached to the term cults (see Miller, 1991).

We will look briefly now at some of the literature on cults and families. Our focus, in this book, is not on cults, but this excursion will hopefully clarify a few points. There is a wealth of scholarly literature available that investigates, at length, this issue which is much broader than our focus and beyond the scope of this book. Our concern is a passing one since our topic of communal families intersects with this much broader issue. In addition, we will look briefly at monasteries and religious orders, two other forms of religious communes, and the Israeli kibbutzim which are predominantly secular communes. Our focus is not specifically on these groups either, but all three of them are communal groups who along with new religious movements have been studied in depth by scholars and they can provide us with some interesting insights. American historians, according to Lawrence McCrank (1997, p. 205), have separated the study of communal and monastic history and we will continue with that policy here, although acknowledging the two are integrally connected. The primary reason we will not be covering the Israeli Kibbutz in depth is that our focus is on American communal utopias. We are commenting on the Kibbutz because it has been one of the most important communal undertakings in the twentieth century and has withstood substantial change in the last several decades, especially regarding the family. These groups also intersect with our topic, but as with cults, a thorough discussion of these communal groups is beyond the scope of this book.

Cults, along with sects, are viewed as deviant religious movements (Stark & Bainbridge, 1985, p. 15). Sects are religious organizations that form to maintain the traditional beliefs and practices of a religious tradition. An example of a sect would be the Old Order Amish. They broke from the Mennonites, another Anabaptist group, to preserve their faith. J. Gordon Melton and Robert L. Moore (1982, p. 17) describe cults as alternative religions and state, "A cult is a religious group that presents a distinctly alternative pattern for doing religion and adhering to a faith perspective than that dominant in the culture."

There has been little research done by social scientists on families within religious movements, while it appears that more attention has been devoted to the members' families of origin and the tension between the cult and the families of origin (Robbins, 1988, p. 51). Thomas Robbins (1988, p. 52) acknowledges that there are some disagreements between researchers regarding whether or not cult development has been assisted by the deterioration of the nuclear family. Some researchers believe family disorganization does not affect a person's decision to join a new religious movement.

Let us look briefly at the Hare Krishna Movement and what Rochford (1996) found regarding family life in that new religious movement. As previously mentioned in Chapter 1, Rochford (1996, p. 153) concluded that the growth in nuclear families reduced member involvement in the movement, but had little effect on the level of member commitment or religiosity.

In the 1960s and early 1970s few members were married, but by 1980 half of the members were married and one fourth had children. By 1992, the majority of members were married and parents. In the early years, ISKCON marriages were usually arranged and family life was very regulated, as was a couple's sex life. Children were required to live in boarding schools away from their parents. By the early 1980s, marital and family life began to change primarily because the economic system of the community was deteriorating. Up until then, ISKCON relied on book and incense sales to support their temples and devotees. Members had to find outside employment to support themselves and ISKCON. This lead to the breakdown of communal living and the development of separate nuclear households (Rochford, 1996, p. 156).

The Hare Krishna are just one of many new religious movements that you might or might not be familiar with (see Daner, 1976, and Shinn, 1987). Arthur S. Parsons (1985) has written a very interesting article on the communal and familial dimensions of the Unification Church, whose members are commonly known as "Moonies." Hall (1990) uses his communal typology discussed earlier in this chapter to analyze Jonestown or more commonly known as "The People's Temple." Hall (1990, p. 271) describes Jonestown as an apocalyptic other-worldly sect. Susan Jean Palmer (1994) enlightens our understanding of the roles women fulfill in new religions by studying the Unification Church, the Hare Krishna, and Rajneesh Movement and there distinct gender patterns. Carl Latkin et al. (1994) share the results of their study of the commune started by Bhagwan Shree Rajneesh in Rajneeshpuram, Oregon which dissolved in 1985. They found that the majority of those surveyed think positively of their past communal experience, even though the commune disbanded amidst turmoil. For those interested in further information on cults and families consult Bromley and Shupe (1981), Kaslow and Sussman (1982), Galanter (1989), and Melton (1992).

As Hillery (1992, p. xxxiii) reminds us, monasteries are the longest-lived communes in history, an often overlooked fact. I will treat monasteries and religious orders as being one in the same. Most religious orders practice some form of communalism and monasteries are populated by specific religious orders. As with communal life in general, there are variations in community life from monastery to monastery, as well as from religious order to religious order.

Is the monastery a family? Hillery (1992, p. 99) cites the responses of a nun who stated that the convent was a family of "mutual adoption," while the famous Trappist monk, Thomas Merton, frequently stated he belonged to a family as well as a community. Hillery (1992, p. 101) concludes that monasteries are not families. Although a kinship model is used to describe relationships (monks refer to each other as brother), Hillery argues that that in and of itself does not create a family. Monasteries have eliminated sexual love, marriage, and sexual relationships. Only the Shakers, according to Hillery (1992, p. xxxiii), have achieved similar success in removing the family. Although, the Shakers are now down to only eight members and monastic membership has also been in decline.

What then holds monastic and religious orders together? Hillery (1992, p. 34) believes it is agape love, one of four types of love and the others being eros, affection, and friendship. One obtains agape love through disciplined freedom. Hillery argues that a monk must learn to love. Relinquishing sexual gratification enables them to move beyond eros or love for an individual and transcend to a broader more universal love, which is agape.

Monastic life is still a viable alternative in today's modern world, a lifestyle that is still relatively unknown and misunderstood. It has garnished some attention in recent years by the success of the Spanish Benedictine Monks of Santo Domingo De Silos and their popular recordings of Gregorian chants and a best-selling book by Kathleen Norris (1996) describing her experiences visiting monasteries. For those interested in pursuing this topic consult Hillery (1992), Ebaugh (1993), McNamara (1996), Wittberg (1994), and a good summary of religious orders and monasteries by McCrank (1997).

It is quite possible that some of you have visited Israel and stayed and maybe even worked on a kibbutz. Many Kibbutzim operate hotels and youth hostels. The Kibbutz has undergone an immense amount of change during the latter part of the twentieth century, particularly in the areas of family and economics. What started back in 1909 as an anti-familialistic, anti-religious, agricultural, collective utopian experiment influenced by Zionism and socialism has blossomed into 270 kibbutzim with approximately 130,000 kibbutzniks (Ben-Rafael, 1997, p. 28).

The egalitarianism which characterized the early and middle years has lessened, while individualism and familism has increased eating at the seams of collectivism. Political changes in the late 1970s brought on by the right-wing Likud party reduced the influence of the kibbutz federations and the worsening economic conditions of many kibbutzim in the mid-1980s has weakened collectivism while increasing privatization (Ben-Rafael, 1997).

The goals of the first generation of kibbutzniks do not carry the same urgency for the third and fourth generations. As families have gained in power and autonomy, the vestiges of the past such as collective dining rooms and children's houses have faded away. Since parents are now responsible for their children and children live in their parent's apartments the community has less control and influence over the children's socialization.

Family ties and family development in the early years of the kibbutz were superseded by communal ties and community development. Four factors supported this arrangement: demographics (more men than women migrated to start kibbutzim), economic organization (communal division of labor), socialist-Zionist ideology (imbued members with a strong communal drive), and military organizations (many kibbutzim were and are military outposts) (Hertz, 1982, p. 30).

One necessary dimension of life that the early kibbutzim did not provide was a substitute for intimacy. Unlike monks and members of religious orders, kibbutzniks did not practice celibacy and agape love was not a substitute for intimacy for them. Therefore, the family began to creep into the kibbutz and as Rosanna Hertz (1982, p. 47) states, "So, community became synonymous with the economy and family became synonymous with intimacy and privacy." As the family gained in ascendancy, so did its authority and influence in the community.

Once outposts in the desert, the kibbutz has evolved and its identity is currently in flux. Many older kibbutzniks are lamenting the "loss of community" which they feel is now occurring; they yearn for the day when gemeinschaft was the focus of kibbutz life. Israel is now a major military and economic power in the Middle East and the kibbutz is no longer an experiment, but a collective which is undergoing growing pains. For more information on the kibbutz movement consult Spiro (1972), Criden and Gelb (1976), Bowes (1989), Hertz (1982), Sturm (1972), Talmon (1973) and Ben-Rafael (1997).

The various cults or new religious movements discussed in this section, such as the Hare Krishna, would easily fit under Kanter's (1972, p. 174) label of service communes. These groups are clearly "creedal" or ideology based groups. The same can be said for the kibbutzim and monasteries. These communes are also service or "creedal" based groups.

Conclusion

Hopefully, this chapter has broadened your understanding of communal living by informing you of the various definitional, conceptual, theoretical, and typological issues related to the study of communal utopias. Communes come in all shapes, sizes, and ideologies. They continue to provide an alternative way of life, as they did in earlier times. Commune, intentional community, and communal utopia are the terms most often used to refer to communal living. While it is difficult to determine the exact number of communal utopias, it is apparent that communal living is as popular in the late 1990s as it was in the 1960s and early 1970s.

Utopian development is connected to millenarian impulses. The mixture of religious, political, and economic factors affects utopian development. While cults (NRMs), monasteries, and the kibbutzim are not the main focus of this book, they are communes. Monasteries, the kibbutzim, and the Hutterites (who will be discussed shortly) alone, account for a large number of communalists worldwide, thus warranting our recognition and attention.

We will be applying both Kanter's theory of commitment and Zablocki's communal types as we discuss past and contemporary communal groups in the United States in the following chapters. Theories and typologies are useful heuristic tools which assist us in our understanding of social phenomenon. Theories are tentative explanations for what scientists have observed and typologies are useful classification schemes. In the next chapter we will look at the Shakers, Oneida, and Amana, three important historic communal utopias.

3

Families in Historic Communal Utopias

Part 1

Three of the better known historic communal utopias are the United Society of Believers in Christ's Second Appearing, otherwise known as the Believers and more popularly known as the Shakers; the Oneida Community, frequently referred to as the Perfectionists; and the Community of True Inspiration, more commonly known as Amana. Although each of these were religious communes, they treated the nuclear family and familial issues differently. As we will see with these three groups and a variety of other communal utopias to be discussed in Chapter 4, family structure and relationships were diverse such as we see among contemporary communal utopias. Some abolished the family unit, substituting celibacy or some other arrangement for monogamy. The vast majority of communal utopias maintained the monogamous family in some type of arrangement with the community.

The Shakers and many of the early American communes adopted celibacy, Oneida created a complex marriage system, while Amana maintained nuclear families, even though theologically they endorsed the moral superiority of celibacy.

The Shakers and the Oneida Community were concerned with eliminating sin and they sought to do so by eradicating the social structures which fostered sin. The Shakers believed the root of sin was sexuality, while the Oneidans believed selfishness in the form of exclusive intimate relationships was the root of sin. Both groups believed changes were required to the institution of the family to eradicate these various sources of sin (Whitworth, 1975, p. 235).

Let us begin our investigation of families among historic communal utopias by looking at the Shakers, the longest-surviving communal group begun in the United States. The Shakers are still practicing communitarians. The Community of True Inspiration, Amana, remains as well, but not as a functioning communitarian group. Their church remains, but they discontinued the communal system in 1931 and formed a joint-stock corporation. Although Amana and the Oneida Community were quite different from one another, they did share one thing in common besides being religious communes. In 1881, 50 years earlier, after disbanding their complex marriage system, the Oneida Community formed a joint-stock company.

The Shakers

The Shakers' story begins in England with Ann Lee (1736-1784), a mystic of working class background, who claimed to have had visions where Jesus Christ appeared and described the sources of evil and misery in the world such as lust, greed, war, and poverty. It was from these visions that Lee, now called Mother Ann by her followers because they believed she was the female counterpart of the Christ spirit or the female Christ, developed her mission in life. William Sims Bainbridge (1997, p. 120) indicates that according to Shaker tradition, Ann Lee believed her own birth in 1736 was the Second Advent. Her mission was to purify and perfect human nature and to free the world of evil and misery, of which abstinence from sex was a prerequisite. Mother Ann was convinced that her concupiscence or lust for sex had led to the eventual deaths of her four children. She believed God had punished her for her sexual desires by the early deaths of her children. Therefore, throughout the remaining years of her life she preached about the necessity of leading a chaste and celibate life (Brewer, 1997, p. 40). The Shakers believed that there would be no sexual relations or carnal motivations in heaven; therefore it would be prudent to adopt celibacy here on earth (Foster, 1981, p. 16).

Mother Ann had a vision in 1772 that influenced her and her small group of followers to leave England in 1774 and journey to America. America was attractive for a variety of reasons and not just to the Shakers. Other European religious groups, especially many German ones such as those who formed Amana, Harmony, Zoar, and the Swedish group who settled Bishop Hill sought the freedom of religious practice that they were denied in many European countries in what would become the United States of America. New England, during the latter 1700s and up through the 1840s, was ripe with religious revivalism and many believed America would be the place of the millennium (McLoughlin, 1978). The Shakers arrived in August and settled in a small community northwest of Albany, New York and primarily out of necessity rather than for religious reasons began to practice communalism.

They were called Shakers because of the way they wiggled, jittered, and gyrated during their religious rituals (see Figure 3.1). Shaker worship in the early years included the Ring Dance which became part of the ritual in 1822. As Edward Horgan describes,

> Four circles were formed with singers at the center. The circles represented the four dispensations of the Shaker faith: to Abraham, Moses, Jesus, and Mother Ann. Females danced in a clockwise motion; males, counterclockwise. Most of the dance patterns were vigorously executed to shake sin and temptation from the body. (Horgan, 1987, p. 74)

Likewise, Lawrence Foster (1981, p. 7) suggests that the transition from monogamy to celibacy was not easy for the Shakers and he states, "The early Shakers often would sing, shout, and dance all night until exhausted, in an attempt to overcome their 'fallen,' carnal natures." Earlier they were referred to as the Shaking Quakers because of Ann Lee's association with some former Quakers in England.

The core beliefs of Shakerism were celibacy, communalism, confession of sin, and separation from the outside world. The Shakers sincerely believed that if they adhered to these principles they could attain perfection. As we will see shortly, the Shakers were not the only group concerned about perfectionism, but they along with the Oneida Com-

Figure 3.1. The Shaker Ring Dance
SOURCE: Collection of the United Society of Shakers, Sabbathday Lake, Maine. Reprinted with permission.

munity were the two who actually enacted this ideology into the social structures of communal life (Brewer, 1997, p. 38).

The Shakers suffered from persecution and prosecution during their first decade in America. Members were beaten and jailed frequently, but they were able to sustain themselves and their fledgling movement. Following the death of Mother Ann in 1784, the Shakers experienced steady growth for approximately 75 years. They created 19 societies in 8 states with some 17,000 members; some Shaker scholars argue that total membership was actually closer to 64,000. James Whittaker followed Mother Ann as leader of the Shakers and upon his death Joseph Meachem ascended to the key leadership position. Meachem appointed Lucy Wright to head the female line of the community and it is generally agreed upon that these two individuals were probably the Shakers' greatest leaders (Kephart & Zellner, 1991, p. 134).

The Shakers believed that the Second Coming had already occurred with the birth of Mother Ann and that their societies had been cleansed of sin (Oved, 1993, p. 42). They believed in the literal interpretation of the Bible and rejected such religious ideas as the Trinity, the immaculate conception, predestination, and the resurrection. They believed God had a male and female counterpart and they also believed in spiritualism—communicating with the dead. Mother Ann is reported to have communicated with certain members regularly, especially during the late 1830s and into the mid-1840s which is attributed to bringing about a spiritual revival among the Shakers (Kephart & Zellner, 1991, p. 152).

There were three stages of membership among the Shakers: (1) the Novitiate Order, (2) the Junior Order, and (3) the Senior Order or Church Order. The Novitiate Order consisted of members who continued to live with their families and owned private property. These members had accepted Shaker beliefs, but did not want to practice communalism. The Junior Order accepted Shaker beliefs and lived in community, while retaining their personal property but not using it. They were full members, but could not become spiritual or economic leaders in the community. The Senior Order or Church Order was the highest level of membership. These Shakers had no personal property, had dissolved all external family ties, and practiced complete communal living. They were considered to be perfect members and according to Shaker theological beliefs, they were already living in heaven. It was from this order that all spiritual and economic leaders were elected and/or appointed to govern the various societies. It is important to realize that even though men and women were treated as equals, the Shakers were not a democracy and that there was a distinct spiritual hierarchy which governed the societies based at the headquarters in New Lebanon, New York and within each of the settlements (Oved, 1993, p. 45).

Even though the Shakers were committed to equality between the sexes in the ecclesiastical world, this was not the case in reference to their ideological foundation (Kern, 1981, p. 289). The Shakers, along with most utopian communities, were proponents of a deep-seated patriarchal ideology. The attack on motherhood, according to Louis Kern, was an attempt by men to control women. The Shakers believed that motherhood was a woman's punishment for her carnal desires and that a life of celibacy would allow women to do away with the curses of motherhood and attain perfection. Kern (1981, p. 290) writes,

The processes of birth and reproduction, the essential female physical functions, were devalued, and male social reproduction (through active conversion and apprenticing orphans), and the rebirth of souls in the dreadness of sin, completely superseded them. Shaker Elders thus assumed the basic functions and prerogatives, in spiritualized and asexual form, of the maternal function.

The Shakers of the mid-1820s were less gemeinschaft in orientation than the founding group and more modern or bureaucratic in their organizational structure (Stein, 1992, p. 133). Prior to Joseph Meacham's rule, the majority of Shakers lived in their own homes, but with the growth the Shakers were experiencing Meacham realized a new social structure was needed to organize the community. It was Meacham who devised the idea of creating families as a means to bring some uniformity and control to the movement (Berry, 1992, p. 33).

Each Shaker community was divided into families which varied in size up to approximately 100 members. Family imagery permeated Shaker life and four kinds of family-related images could be found among the Shakers: family, home, parent-child relations, and brother-sister relations (Lauer & Lauer, 1983b, p. 218). What was once the nuclear family became the communal family, communities were viewed as homes, Mother Ann was the parent and the brothers and sisters were her children, and men and women were brothers and sisters because they had a common mother, Ann Lee. Shaker songs were replete with these images. Each family was headed by two elders and two eldresses, deacons and deaconesses, and trustees. The elders and eldresses supervised the spiritual life of the community and replaced the biological fathers and mothers, deacons and deaconesses handled everyday affairs, while trustees coordinated business matters both in and outside of the community. Men and women shared the leadership responsibilities within the communities, but the division of labor was regulated along gender lines. Jeanette C. Lauer and Robert H. Lauer (1983a, p. 23) credit the Shakers, along with Oneida, as having the least sexual division of labor among the nineteenth-century communal societies. Men did the farming, construction, furniture manufacturing, etc., while women fulfilled the traditional roles in the kitchen, housework such as cleaning, and the washing and mending of clothes, etc. In essence, the families functioned as traditional monogamous families minus the sexual connection. Although the Shakers tried to maintain order and uniformity within their various societies, the families were never identical because of the unique composition of their members.

Although the Shakers abolished the nuclear family unit, they did not abolish family functions outside of sexual relations. Members had to separate from their nuclear or natural family and join and become integrated into a Shaker family. Those who were married when they joined had to live as brother and sister not as husband and wife, but they were not separated by one living in one society and the other sent to another society. They were allowed to stay within the same society. Brewer (1986, p. 69) relates that it was typical for the Shakers to reside in families where one third to one half of the members were biologically related. She found, for example, that in the Hancock Church Family that over one half of its members came from five extended families. Another familial aspect which was retained was that of affection. Affection was to be shared with all members not just former spouses, siblings, or parents (Bainbridge, 1997, p. 129).

Because the Shakers renounced sex and marriage they tried to segregate men and women as often as possible to reduce physical contact of any kind including shaking hands and touching, which was prohibited. The brothers and sisters slept in different rooms, which were located on opposite sides of the building. Many of the buildings had separate entrances for each sex as well as separate staircases so members would not be able to brush up against each other. They ate at separate tables, a custom that the monogamous Hutterites still practice. Brothers and sisters were not allowed to be alone with each other unless there was a third adult present (Kephart & Zellner, 1991, p. 143).

Boys and girls, whether they were the sons and daughters of members or orphans the community took in, were also subjected to the same separation rules. The boys were supervised by the brothers and the girls were supervised by the sisters. Kephart and Zellner (1991, p. 144) indicate that it was possible that a young Shaker boy or girl could live their whole life as a Shaker and never be touched by a member of the opposite sex.

Although brothers and sisters were separated on most occasions, there were times during the week where they could talk and enjoy each other's company. These encounters were called union meetings. A number of brothers would be seated across from a number of sisters and they were allowed to converse about a variety of topics including Shaker theology, daily affairs, and sometimes the group even sang. In addition, each brother was assigned a sister who cleaned and mended his clothes and performed other domestic types of services, while he would be available to assist her in doing manual labor types of tasks which she might not be able to do (Kephart & Zellner, 1991, p. 144).

Shaker families had their fair share of an occasional misunderstanding or two among members, but overall the families exhibited a great deal of harmony (Brewer, 1986, p. 70). As one might suspect, the Shakers were not totally successful in controlling emotional and physical relationships between brothers and sisters. While they were not allowed to give or receive gifts for fear that this act might endear one member to another, it was not unheard of for couples to leave and marry as a result of the contacts developed in the union meetings (Muncy, 1973, p. 41).

Women were usually overrepresented within the various Shaker societies. Part of the reason for this is explained by Theologian Marjorie Procter-Smith (1985, p. 220),

> The Shaker system was seen to be the best solution to the problems of women in the world, and for many women, it doubtless was. Life in a Shaker society offered economic security, meaningful activity, and a supportive sisterhood; for a few women, it offered the opportunity to exercise gifts of leadership which would hardly have been tolerated in the outside world or in any other religious institution.

Celibacy and communal child-rearing practices, according to Foster (1991, p. 31), gave Shaker women more freedom and opportunity to pursue other interests, especially for leadership roles within the societies. Since women were freed from the obligations of the outside world and earthly marriage, they were able to devote themselves fully to God, and from the Shakers' point of view women could therefore devote themselves to the needs of their communal families.

If life for the Shakers was, in most cases, idyllic, what contributed to the decline of such a once successful utopian movement? Shaker membership started to decline after the Civil War and by the beginning of the twentieth-century Shaker communities were closing. Several reasons have been offered for their decline. The economy was changing and mass production was replacing the hand work that provided labor for the Shakers. Economic mismanagement put more and more of the Shaker societies into debt. Better transportation and communication opened up the world to young Shakers. The families were not receiving as many orphans as before and for a celibate group, this was a necessary source of potential adult members. A major reason for the decline of not just the Shakers, but other celibate groups was the changing attitude about sex. Fewer people viewed sex as dirty and sinful. Victorianism and Puritanism no longer had the influence they once did over sexuality. Industrialization and urbanization, outcomes of modernity, provided people with many more options and choices than they ever had before. This as well as the changing attitudes about sex set in motion the decline of the Shakers (Kephart & Zellner, 1991, p. 154).

Which of Kanter's (1972) commitment mechanisms were used by the Shakers to enhance their structural arrangements and organizational strategies or in the words of Etzioni (1996) what activities developed layered loyalties between individuals and the community? Edward W. Hassinger and James R. Pinkerton (1986, p. 383) found that Shakers employed all six types of commitment building mechanisms in their societies and families.

Celibacy was the major form of sacrifice exhibited by the Shakers and, to some degree, they led a less materialistic lifestyle then they could have. Investment was high especially for those who entered the Senior or Church Order. Their assets were turned over to the community and would be returned if they left permanently. Renunciation was important and the Shakers placed a great deal of emphasis on withdrawing from the world and renouncing personal and nuclear family relationships. Probably the major form of renunciation was the elimination of the nuclear family, but as we have seen the family was recreated as a communal family which provided nurturance and a sense of intimacy for the Shakers. Communion held the Shakers together. Communal work, worship, property, the focus on sharing within the communities and families all strengthened their repose. Another valuable factor and one that Hall (1988) identified was that the Shakers shared similar ethnic and religious backgrounds. Confession was an important form of mortification practiced by the Shakers. Members were expected to confess their sins to their elders or eldressess. Shaker life transcended the normal everyday affairs because they believed the end of the world was near and their attention was focused on preparing for it, that is one reason why they were not concerned about procreation.

There are only eight Shakers residing at Sabbathday Lake, Maine, the last functioning Shaker society—the same number of people who accompanied Ann Lee from England. A Shaker eldress, shortly before her death, stated in a video documentary done in the late 1980s, that there was some significance that the once prosperous and numerous Shakers had been reduced to the same number of members that Mother Ann started with in the late 1700s. The eldress cited some prophecy from Mother Ann which foresaw this decline, but Mother Ann predicted that the Shakers would be rejuvenated and come back stronger than ever. Time will be the judge of that prophecy.

The Oneida Community

While the Shakers shunned sex, the Oneida Community invented, what some would call, a radical approach to sexual relationships. Unlike the Shakers, the Oneidans believed that God approved of sexual relationships, therefore the act was not sinful. They believed people had sex both on earth and in heaven (Muncy, 1973, p. 168). The Oneida Community found monogamy restricting and practiced pantagamy. Pantagamy is found in communities where every woman is considered the wife of every man and every man is considered the husband of every woman. This is not to be confused with polygamy, which was practiced by the Mormons and still is today by some Mormon sects not affiliated with The Church of Jesus Christ of Latter-Day Saints based in Salt Lake City, Utah. It is not surprising then, that the early utopian groups in the United States were viewed with more than just a passing curiosity. The Shakers practiced celibacy, the Mormons practiced polygamy, and the Oneidans practiced pantagamy. All three of these groups and many other communal utopias were rejecting monogamy for nontraditional family forms. Pantagamy is not the only radical issue that brought attention to the Oneida Community, but before we address these additional issues, let us begin with a discussion of John Humphrey Noyes, the founder of the Oneida Community.

John Humphrey Noyes was born in 1811 in Vermont and eventually graduated from Dartmouth College. He was swept up in the religious revivalism of that era and in 1833 received a license from the Yale Divinity School to preach. Soon thereafter, Noyes claimed he was sinless and Yale revoked his license. Noyes preached that Christ had already returned to earth, therefore man was already redeemed from sin and could under the appropriate circumstances lead a perfect and sinless life. Noyes was preaching an extreme form of Christianity known as Perfectionism that emphasized self-perfection and communalism (Kephart & Zellner, 1994, p. 51).

Like the Shakers, the Oneida Community at first did not practice communal living and consisted of members of his family including two sisters, a brother, and his mother. Others joined and by 1844 they began to live communally. By 1846, they started experimenting with group marriage, essentially the sharing of spouses and 1848 marked the official founding of the Oneida Community, located in Oneida, New York. There were 87 members living communally in 1848, by 1849 that number more than doubled. The community had 300 members at its peak. In the summer of 1849, the Mansion House was completed. This building became the center of life for the community and contained a communal dining hall, sleeping rooms, library, recreation rooms, etc. (Kephart & Zellner, 1994, p. 53).

The Oneida Community is unique for a variety of reasons directly related to their rejection of monogamy, but they are also unique because they were the first group of utopians born solely in the United States. Their ideology was not based on European sectarianism and their founder was not an immigrant (Oved, 1993, p. 167).

The Oneidans did not maintain a church or hold prayer services, communion services, baptisms, weddings, or even funerals. Although they did away with the formal vestiges or trappings of religion, the religion was integrated into their everyday life. They read the Bible and discussed it and more importantly, they believed that by living a life of self-perfection and communalism they were being religious (Kephart & Zellner, 1994, p. 57). While they read and discussed the Bible, Noyes's views of it, according to Maren Lockwood Carden (1971, p. 1), were controversial, "He taught that one should follow only the inspired spirit of the Bible, not the letter of its law. To him, there were no absolute standards of morality." The theology developed by Noyes was very similar to that of the Shakers except Noyes believed the kingdom of heaven was available in this world to those who practiced his version of Perfectionism (Muncy, 1973, p. 162).

There were three key principles which governed life within the Oneida Community: complex marriage, male continence, and mutual criticism (Berry, 1992, p. 96). Noyes asserted that the kingdom of heaven was attainable on earth by controlling individualism and the attention given to fulfilling one's needs and wants. He believed that if individual desires and wishes were subordinated to those of the larger community, true perfection could be obtained and this could be best accomplished by eliminating the monogamous family and by creating an enlarged family. Complex marriage, male continence, and mutual criticism were the practices which helped them achieve the kingdom of heaven on earth (Foster, 1997, p. 257).

Male continence and mutual criticism facilitated the development of complex marriage. Male continence or coitus reservatus was a form of birth control that Noyes incorporated into the sex life of his community. He believed ejaculation was not necessary for men and that with practice and forbearance a man could enjoy sexual relations without attaining a climax, while at the same time male continence relieved women of the burden of unwanted pregnancies (Kephart & Zellner, 1994, p. 53). Male continence was not 100% effective. As many as 30 children were conceived unintentionally during the first 20 years of the community (Muncy, 1973, p. 183).

Mutual criticism was believed to bring about self-improvement by subjecting oneself to the criticism of others. Members were criticized for their lack of spirituality and/or for their individualism or even sexual matters. All members were open to criticism except John Humphrey Noyes. This activity enhanced individual morale and group cohesion, although it goes without saying that for many members, mutual criticism must have been painful at times (Kephart & Zellner, 1994, p. 65).

Male continence and mutual criticism were forms of social control which prepared the members for the adoption of complex marriage. Male continence provided some security that the sexual liberation experienced by community members would not result in overpopulation, while mutual criticism restricted the passions of members and provided a system of checks and balances for the practice of complex marriage (Muncy, 1973, p. 184). Noyes believed that group marriage was superior to monogamous marriage because it eliminated selfishness and romantic love, both viewed as destructive because Noyes preached it was, "Natural for all men to love all women, and for all women to love all men" (Kephart & Zellner, 1994, p. 74). Romantic love was an exclusive love which eliminated others from the dyad or monogamous relationship, while complex marriage or group marriage propagated inclusive love.

To encourage complex marriage, as well as to facilitate its smooth functioning, the community implemented a go-between system. Usually an older woman would act as a liaison between the party requesting sex and the party being requested to have sex. The go-between reduced the potential unpleasantness that might accompany a refusal or excuse for not wanting sex. The go-between also helped to keep tract if exclusive relationships were developing. If this was the case, the community could then intervene and break up the potentially harmful relationship (Kephart & Zellner, 1994, p. 77).

A crucial ingredient of complex marriage was the principle of ascending fellowship. Noyes believed there was an inherent order of perfectionism at Oneida and that members were ranked from low to high based on their level of perfection. Those members wishing to improve their standing in the community and self-perfection were encouraged to associate with those who were spiritually higher up the ladder within the community. In most cases, those who were higher up the ladder spiritually were the older members of the community. Therefore what ensued was that younger women and older men and younger men and older woman paired off sexually. Young sexually active men were already accustomed to being with older postmenopausal women while they were learning male continence. Noyes and several of the other higher ranking older men introduced the young women to their first experience of sexual intercourse. By this time, older men had mastered male continence and the chances were quite reduced that these young women would become pregnant (Carden, 1971, p. 52).

For about 20 years from 1848 to 1868 members of Oneida did not bear children. This policy was not popular so it was rescinded in 1868 and Oneida began a program called stirpiculture. This program allowed only certain members of the community to become parents. They were selected by a committee of their brethren who picked prospective parents based on their level of self-perfection and later on physical condition. The purpose of this eugenics program was to develop a superior or perfected human being. Approximately one fourth of the parents were selected by the committee and the remaining three fourths who became parents applied to the committee as a couple. Of the 41 stirpiculture children who were born between 1869 and 1879, Noyes fathered 10 of them (Carden, 1971, p. 63).

Child rearing was a community affair at Oneida. Noyes taught that all children should love all adults and vice versa, just as all adults were to love each other. Young children stayed with their mothers until they were 15 months old, then they lived with all the other Oneida children under the age of 12 in the Children's House. The children spent little time with their biological parents because the community feared that a special love would develop which would further separate them from other communal members. The children were educated within the community and the older children spent 1 hour each day working on the communal farm or in one of the community business enterprises. Most of the children took turns sleeping in the rooms of adult members, each member had their own room. The children were rotated frequently so no special relationships would form. One of the advantages of the communal family was that childless adults could become active communal parents (Carden, 1971, p. 63).

Although the focus of Oneida was on the communal family, nuclear families were also recognized. In 1873 there were four, four-generation biological families and ten, three-generation families residing at the Mansion House. Noyes's family dominated community life from the early years to the end. Women who were married upon joining Oneida were referred to as Mrs. *(surname of her husband)*. Biological parents chose the name of their offspring. Nuclear and communal families coexisted for the duration of the community and as Marlyn Klee-Hartzell (1996, p. 20) states,

> It is striking to note the extent to which a recognition of the nuclear family persisted throughout the Oneida Community's history. In the last decade of its existence, as the communal fabric began to unravel, Community members staged mock weddings and younger members competed to get

permission to have stirpiculture children with their secret, favored lovers. Eventually, some young women refused to have sex with men, and expressed their desire for monogamous marriages and nuclear families. Although the communal family was the ideal at Oneida, the reality fell far short.

After Oneida disbanded and formed a joint-stock company in 1881, many husbands and wives reunited, while others became legally married. Children were adopted and some mothers remained unmarried (Klee-Hartzell, 1996, p. 22).

Noyes's philosophy called for the elimination of all distinctions between men and women in economic life that were not intrinsic and he believed there were few of them. Men and women worked alongside one another and some women were in positions of authority over men (Foster, 1981, p. 232). As long as his followers paid him the homage he felt due which reinforced his paternalistic God-like ways, he worked toward equality between the sexes.

Rather than using gender as the criterion for one's position and duties, Oneida was governed by the principle of ascending and descending fellowship (Foster, 1991, p. 96). Ellen Wayland-Smith (1988, p. 50) argues that based on the diaries and other writings of community members, women at Oneida were neither privileged nor subordinated in the positions they held. There were not significant differences regarding the status of men and women, but that does not mean that everyone was liberated. The power and authority of Noyes, she argues, limited freedom and liberation for both men and women.

What brought about the dissolution of Oneida? The dismantling of complex marriage and the departure of Noyes, both in 1879, shook the community (Muncy, 1973, p. 195). Even though Oneida was a successful community for more than 25 years, they experienced both internal and external conflict which eventually brought the community to cease communal living in 1881. As Noyes aged, he played less of a role in managing the community and a group of Oneidans rose to challenge him. This produced a significant amount of turmoil which the community never recovered from. There was also some unrest regarding who was chosen for the stirpiculture experiments as well as who would initiate young virgins. In addition to these internal pressures, the community was being criticized by several outside sources for their alternative lifestyle and sexual practices (Foster, 1988, p. 13).

On January 1, 1881, after much discussion and planning the Oneida Community became a joint-stock company called the Oneida Limited. Former members received shares of stock in the company. Readers might be familiar with this company because of its reputation for fine silverware, cooper wire, and cooking utensils (Kephart & Zellner, 1994, p. 91).

Before we move on to a discussion of Amana and some of the other German Pietist groups, let us look again at Kanter's (1972) commitment mechanisms and apply them to Oneida. We will not be applying her mechanisms to every group we study, but since Oneida was in existence for a lengthy period of time they warrant our attention.

In comparison with the Shakers, the Oneidans did not sacrifice as much and they were certainly not as austere as the Shakers. The Oneidans did invest their labor and assets in the community, but if they left they were able to take with them an amount equal to what they invested. Even members who invested no property or other assets were given $100.00 when they left Oneida. Renunciation did play an important role for the community. The Mansion House and other community owned facilities provided the members with all they needed and they rarely left, although they were free to do so. Communion was supported primarily by the emphasis on sharing in the everyday life of the community. Complex marriage as well as the communal enterprises and the homogeneity of members fostered communion. Communion was also strengthened by the persecution experience of the early Oneidans while the community was forming in Vermont. Mutual criticism played a major role in the community and was a form of mortification. Oneida was a community based on transcendence. They believed Noyes was divinely inspired and that through complex marriage and the philosophy of ascending fellowship, they were reaping the rewards of heaven on earth (Hassinger & Pinkerton, 1986, p. 389).

The Shakers and Oneida are viewed as being more radical in how they dealt with nuclear families. Amana, as we will see, maintained nuclear families and flourished. They too, eventually succumbed to the changing times. I selected the Shakers, Oneida, and Amana for study because they represent a variety of positions on the familistic scale, from the abolishment of nuclear families, to creating a new family form, to maintaining nuclear families.

Amana

The Community of True Inspiration is noteworthy for several reasons, but none more important than it was the fourth longest-surviving communal society in the history of the United States. Only the Shakers, the Hutterites, and the Rappites existed longer as communal utopias. Amana, as a religious organization, will be celebrating its 300-year anniversary in 2014. It was a communal society for 89 years and has been a community for over 150 years. By 1932, Amana had divided into two separate units—the Amana Society, a joint-stock corporation, and the Amana Church Society, both of which are still in existence today. Let us now look back in history to the beginning of the 18th century and the start of what was to become the Community of True Inspiration (Andelson, 1997, p. 201).

The Community of True Inspiration began in 1714, in Germany, as a Pietist sect which rejected the authority of the Lutheran Church. They believed that God should be worshipped through the thoughtful reflection of Scripture, not by arguing specific and often arcane theological points of view. They believed the Church intellectualized worship too much and they preferred, as did other Pietists, that worship services reflect more of a simple less formal, more emotional and direct approach to communicating with God. This type of worship was thought to be more conducive when done in small groups. Thus, those Pietists who separated from the Church and formed small groups were called Separatists (Andelson, 1997, p. 183; Grossmann, 1984).

The Separatists came primarily from the peasant and lower middle classes and they believed in biblical prophecies and that God spoke through individuals who were called instruments. In its early years, the community was led by two *Werkzeuge* (instruments), Eberhard Ludwig Gruber and Johann Frederick Rock. As the group grew and extended its influence into other areas of Germany, the Lutheran Church and secular authorities began to persecute the Separatists. During this period of persecution, the instruments died and no one followed to take their places until 1817. The religious community struggled during this period until Michael Krausert, Christian Metz, and Barbara Heineman emerged as instruments. Metz and 320 Separatists, influenced by a series of prophecies, immigrated to the United States in 1843 and settled near Buffalo, New York (Oved, 1993, p. 87).

Their first community was called Ebenezer and eventually there were four settlements which adopted a modified form of communalism amidst a call for privatization by some of the more affluent members. These dissenters were thrown out of the community. The leaders of the community were fearful if privatization prevailed it would slowly ruin the religious community. All was not well though, the Ebenezer communes experienced problems with their neighbors, the Seneca Indians, regarding land. Metz and other leaders also wanted to move to a more isolated area where members would not be tempted by the evils of city life. By 1854, Metz had received another message from the Holy Spirit to relocate the Separatists west (Berry, 1992, p. 53).

By the summer of 1855, the Inspirationists moved to eastern Iowa and named their community Amana after a biblical location, a mountain peak, from the Song of Solomon. Eventually they created seven settlements amassing 26,000 acres of excellent farm land and timber (Andelson, 1985b, p. 34). The economy was based on farming and manufacturing, they were known for the quality of their products, especially woolen items. Young people began working after they had completed the eighth grade, usually at age 14. A board of elders assigned them a position in one of the communal enterprises. Women worked in traditional roles, such as in the communal kitchens and gardens, while there were more options for men. The various colonies were governed by a 13-member Great Council, who were all men, elected annually by the adult men (over 21 years old) and women (over 30 years old) (Andelson, 1997, p. 190).

According to Bertha M. H. Shambaugh (1988, p. 137),

It is the institution of the family that has been the salvation of the Community of True Inspiration. It is clear that the far-sighted Christian Metz perceived this long before his less "highly endowed and especially favored Brothers." Without it the growth of the Community would practically have stopped with the last accessions from Germany.

Shambaugh's statement is a concise and revealing piece of evidence, especially in light of some recent research done by Jonathan G. Andelson (1985a, p. 23). Inspirationists had a much higher rate of celibacy than other Europeans. For example, for those Inspirationists born between 1800 and 1840, 50% remained celibate. Celibacy was a matter of religion for them, as it was for other groups like the Shakers, and they believed it was a special gift from God which elevated one spiritually. Utopian communities, including the Inspirationists, looked to Scripture for guidance and they found the admonition encouraging celibacy in the writings attributed to the Apostle Paul in I Corinthians 7:38 (Andelson, 1985a, p. 4).

Why then did fewer and fewer Inspirationists elect a life of celibacy and why did the family gain in prominence? The answers to these questions are complicated, but the main reason is that once the Inspirationists immigrated to the United States the celibacy rate dropped drastically among both those born within the community and those who joined from outside the community. It appears the community was not as successful in inculcating the value of celibacy to its new members. Also, by the time the Inspirationists had relocated to Iowa, the revivalistic movement in the United States had waned. Another important factor is that more and more of the elders, who were expected to remain single, and other important leaders in the various settlements began to marry, especially after the death of Metz. Another reason is that a large number of Saxons who emigrated in the 1880s and joined Amana had very low rates of celibacy (Andelson, 1985a, p. 27).

As Oved (1993, p. 416) observes,

> Amana, which had the same background as Harmony and other communes in the eighteenth century, was motivated by a theology that supported the moral superiority of celibacy. However, the realistic approach of its founders prompted them to maintain the family and thereby ensure their growth and survival.

Oved and Shambaugh both make very valid points. One only has to look to the Shakers to see what happened to membership when celibacy no longer was viewed as a desirable lifestyle. The Inspirationists were pragmatists at heart.

Amana was one of the largest and most successful communal utopias which allowed familism, even though the Inspirationists did not encourage marriage and elevated celibacy over marital sexual relationships. The elders, especially in the early years in the United States, made it difficult for members to marry. Men had to be at least 24 and women at least 20 before they could marry, and one was not allowed to marry a non-Inspirationist. Couples who planned to marry had to get the permission of the Werkzeuge and the Great Council and they were reminded that if permission was granted for them to marry their social standing in the society, especially within the Church, would decrease. Another interesting custom was that the young man was forced to relocate to another Inspirationist settlement for one full year and during this time he could not see his future bride. Once this year had passed, he could see his future bride every other Sunday after Church services. If they both still wanted to marry they then appeared before the *Werkzeuge* and the Great Council and a decision was then made whether they would be allowed to marry (Muncy, 1973, p. 97).

Weddings at Amana, according to Muncy (1973, p. 99), were more like funerals. Although Barthel (1984, p. 53) writes that by the early 1900s, weddings were more joyous and they became a communal feast, instead of a private affair in the home of the bride. The newlyweds still could not be together; it was required that the groom return to the village where he had spent the previous year. He could return to his wife in 2 weeks. At that time the Council would assign them a place to live, usually with either of their parents. They would be given a bedroom with single beds, the message being that having children was not encouraged by the society. As with marriage, childbirth brought a downward realignment of the couple's social position in the society (Muncy, 1973, p. 99). Pregnant women had to dress in such a manner as to conceal their pregnancy. Although marriage and childrearing were discouraged, families with four children were typical, while those families with seven or eight children were called "rabbit families" (Barthel, 1984, p. 55).

Families lived in buildings owned by the society; two or three families shared a house where each family was designated a certain number of bedrooms depending on the size of their family. These houses only contained bedrooms and sitting rooms. Kitchens and communal dining rooms where located in the center of a group of communal houses. From 30 to 40 people were served three meals daily cooked by the women from the nearby homes. Men and women dined at separate tables which was another measure to control the influence of families (Muncy, 1973, p. 100). Every family was provided credit (a fixed amount annually) at the colony store for personal items including clothing, shoes, and other goods. Since Amana was a communal operation where resources and income were pulled together, the society paid for the upkeep of its members and property. If someone needed to see a physician one was provided. Amanans were cared for by the community from cradle to grave.

As Muncy (1973, p. 100) states, "Precautions were taken at Amana to keep the sexes apart from a very early age." Young men were encouraged to stay away from young women, and even when young people were out walking, girls were to walk in one direction and boys in the other to avoid contact. Barthel (1984, p. 55) comments that the influence of the family and the opposite sex was also tempered by the fact that the majority of the day was spent in work which was segregated by sex as well. The sexes were also separated at Church, men entered and existed through one door and women through another and once inside they sat away from one another (Muncy, 1973, p. 101).

The extended family was a valuable resource especially regarding child care, but it could also be restrictive and controlling (Barthel, 1984, p. 45). Everyone knew everyone else and of course, they knew their personal business too. There was also a *Kinderschule* or child care center provided by the community. Children were educated by the society up through the eighth grade. A few of the brightest children, who were usually from prominent families, were sent on for training as doctors, dentists, and teachers.

Although the customs, rules, and regulations at Amana might appear to have been repressive, families survived and Amana lost very few of its young people to the outside world. Muncy (1973, p. 101) contends that the community provided peace and security which was more than enough to keep the young people "on the farm." While this might have been the case, Barthel (1984, p. 54) found that the family remained strong, even in light of the bias against it, and was one source of contention and division throughout the life of the society.

If the society was retaining the majority of its young people, what then contributed to the reorganization of Amana? Did Amana lack the layered loyalties we have discussed in Chapter 1 that are so vital and necessary for a group to survive? Families, as Shambaugh remarked, saved the Community of True Inspiration from extinction once the community immigrated to America and eventually to Iowa, but were families possibly a dual-edged sword staving off extinction to reappear as the villain in later years?

As we have seen, Amana was successful for a long period of time in incorporating families into the communal structure, albeit reluctantly, but Andelson (1997, p. 193) concludes that eventually a growing number of Inspirationists were tired of all the rules and regulations governing communal life. They wanted more freedom and the ability to increase their material consumption and their standard of living. There was growing discontent regarding the influence certain people had in the society. The perception was that larger families were discriminated against and that certain families held more of the prestigious positions in the society. Since the community only sent a few of its young people on for higher education, many felt passed over or limited in what was open for them within the society.

By the 1880s, apostasy rates increased and beginning in 1905 there was a steady decline in population. To make matters even worse, Amana was experiencing economic troubles. Their clothing business experienced a setback due to World War I and never recovered. During the 1920s they experienced several devastating fires which gutted their woolen mills. They did not have insurance and suffered huge losses in property and machinery.

To compound these already negative problems, the stock market crash of October of 1929 was the nail which sealed the death notice of Amana (Andelson, 1997, p. 196).

Communal ownership appeared, to many people, to be the source of the trouble in the Amana Colonies. In 1931, a committee appointed by the Great Council created a questionnaire with only two questions which were to be answered by the 917 adult members. The first question asked whether or not the respondent and his or her family was willing to return to the old lifestyle of the original Inspirationists, while the second question asked them if they were willing to support a reorganization of the community into a joint-stock corporation and a Church Society. The respondents supported the reorganization proposal. The communal businesses were therefore, taken over by the joint-stock corporation in 1932 and individuals and families became stockholders (Andelson, 1997, p. 196).

Andelson (1997, p. 197) speculates that possibly the "Great Change," as it was called, was not needed after all. Changes could have been made in operating procedures and unprofitable businesses could have been closed. Close scrutiny of the questionnaires completed by members in 1931 revealed that depending on how the responses were interpreted, more than a third and possibly almost one half of the respondents were supportive of the old communal system. Economic problems helped to bring about the reorganization of Amana, but they were only part of the reason.

Returning to one of our original questions, did the nuclear families contribute to the downfall of the communal way of life? Yes, they did in part contribute to the downfall, but they were only partly to blame. The jealousy that was spread throughout the community was linked to family life. It appears that a vocal and more powerful segment of Inspirationists were unwilling to continue living communally and they became the piece of straw which broke the camel's back. No doubt, modernity played a part in this drama by competing with the Gemeinschaft value system of Amana. The layered loyalties of peace and security were not enough to stem the tide of change in Amana. As with most things in life, it is usually a combination of factors which leads to major changes and restructuring.

Conclusion

The Shakers, Oneida, and Amana were each influenced by strong charismatic leaders: Mother Ann Lee founder of the Shakers, John Humphrey Noyes founder of Oneida, and a string of *Werkzeuge* (instruments) who guided Amana including Eberhard Ludwig Gruber, Johann Frederick Rock, Michael Krausert, Christian Metz, and Barbara Heineman. While charisma, alone, is not enough to hold a community together, it is a necessary ingredient, especially in religious communes as these three communal utopias attest to.

The Shakers shunned sex, although the transition from monogamy to celibacy was fraught with tension for some. Celibacy, communalism, confession of sin, and separation from the outside world were the tools which the Shakers thought would enable them to achieve perfection. The community was based on a spiritual hierarchy and Shaker life was permeated with family imagery, although at its roots it was still very patriarchal.

While the Shakers shunned sex, Oneida embraced it. They practiced pantagamy. After a period of about 20 years of childlessness, children were allowed and they were raised by the community. Noyes believed the kingdom of heaven was available to those who practiced his version of Perfectionism (complex marriage, male continence, and mutual criticism).

Amana, like the Shakers, believed in the value of celibacy, but unlike the Shakers, they were not able to institute its practice. They tried to keep men and women apart as much as possible, as did the Shakers. While the community exerted a lot of control over newlyweds, the young married couple eventually became integrated into the activity of daily communal life. Amana was one of the largest and most successful communal utopias of all time which allowed nuclear families.

In the next chapter, we will discuss Ephrata, Harmony (The Rappites), and Zoar. All of these groups practiced celibacy. We will also investigate Icaria, the Fourierist Phalanxes, and Bishop Hill, who maintained monogamous nuclear families, and the Mormons who practiced polygamy.

In addition to these groups, we will investigate the Hutterites who trace their practice of community of goods back to 1528 in Europe. The Hutterites are an Anabaptist religious group who eventually migrated from Russia to what is now South Dakota in 1874 and they continue to thrive today. Although the Hutterites arrived on the American scene later than other historic communal utopias, their long history is dotted with episodes of communitarianism. While thoroughly communitarian in design, they have successfully maintained the nuclear family. William Kephart (1982, p. 279) states,

> In fact, of the scores of communistic groups that have appeared on the North American scene, the Hutterian Brethren are far and away the most successful. Most of the others have either changed their economic orientation or are now defunct.

4

Families in Historic Communal Utopias

Part 2

Although all three were religious communal utopias, the Shakers, Oneida, and Amana dealt with marriage and family life in different ways. While frequently less known in comparison to the Shakers, Oneida, and Amana, the following historic communal utopias also struggled with the question of community versus family. Let us now continue with our discussion of family life in historic communes.

The Ephrata Cloister was founded by Conrad Beissel in 1732 in Pennsylvania. Beissel had belonged to the Brethren movement, but broke from them because they would not follow his views which included celibacy, Saturday, not Sunday as the Sabbath, and dietary laws from the Old Testament. Beissel stated that these positions were made known to him through revelations from heaven. Eventually a group of celibate men and women joined him and formed a monastic community. In addition to these men and women, another group called householders became members of Ephrata Cloister. The householders consisted of two groups: those who lived together and had children and those couples who shared a household, but refrained from sexual relations (Durnbaugh, 1997, p. 23).

Those couples who were not celibate resided in homes nearby the others. There was a clear separation between the brothers and sisters who lived the monastic life and those householders who were viewed as secular. The celibates were believed to be perfect, while the others were lower on the spiritual hierarchy, even though they participated in the religious rituals and economic undertakings of the community (Oved, 1993, p. 26).

The Ephrata Cloister was known for their printing, calligraphy, music, and manuscript illumination. Beissel died in 1768 and Peter Miller assumed the reigns of leadership. Ephrata began to falter as the result of a typhoid epidemic which wiped out nearly one third of the brothers and sisters. The community never recouped after the epidemic and in 1786 private ownership of goods was introduced (Oved, 1993, p. 32). The Cloister ended in 1814 and was succeeded by the Society of Seventh Day Baptists. A daughter colony by the name of Snow Hill had been formed in 1798 and existed until 1889. Families which were members of these groups formed the German Seventh Day Baptist Church (Durnbaugh, 1997, p. 26).

George Rapp broke from the Lutheran Church, in Germany in 1785, and by 1805 Rapp and his followers, who were known as the Rappites, had settled in what was to become Harmony, Pennsylvania, not far from Pittsburgh. The Harmony Society was based on three beliefs: community of goods, millennialism, and sexual abstinence. The Rappites believed even sexual intercourse in marriage was sinful. Each family had their own house, livestock, and gardens and were able to acquire whatever else they needed from Society stores and enterprises. Each family had an account from which they could draw to purchase these additional goods and services (Arndt, 1997, p. 60).

The Harmony Society experienced a revival during 1807 and 1808 and Rapp, as their spiritual leader, determined that Christ's Second Coming was near. It was at this time that they adopted celibacy. Those already married were ordered to give up sex and future marriages were discouraged. Berry (1992, p. 45) comments that celibacy was not totally for religious reasons, celibacy served social and economic purposes too. Mothers could not participate in the work force and children consumed food. By eliminating childbirth, women could be fully integrated into the work force and there would be fewer mouths to feed. The community relocated to southern Indiana and created a prosperous village called New Harmony. Despite their success in taming the wilderness, Rapp moved the community back to Pennsylvania and sold the New Harmony properties to Robert Owen who developed his own utopian society there from 1825 to 1827. The Rappites settled in what became known as Economy (Arndt, 1997, p. 74).

Celibacy became an issue again and those not succumbing to sexual abstinence were thrown out of the community. The Rappites prospered in Economy and the community became quite wealthy, but that was not enough to stem the gradual deterioration of Economy. The millennium failed to come and celibacy was not a popular way of life, so by 1832 the community experienced a schism which further weakened them. By 1905, the Harmony Society had dissolved (Arndt, 1997, p. 81).

German Separatists, like the Rappites and the Community of True Inspiration, were joined by others including the Separatists of Zoar. The spiritual leader of Zoar was Joseph Baumler and the name of the community came from the Book of Genesis 19:22, Zoar was the biblical town to which Lot retreated. The community of Zoar, like other Separatist groups, was millennial and they practiced celibacy. They believed they were an oasis in a desert of sin and immorality. They settled in Ohio in 1819 and started to practice community of goods. Zoar was like many of the other pietist and separatist sects of that era, they did not originally intend to live communally, but out of economic necessity it was prudent for them to pool their resources. Their original intention was to be solely a religious group (Berry, 1992, p. 50).

The community abandoned celibacy in 1830 primarily because they were never truly committed to it and most members returned to a monogamous married life. Families played an important role in community life. Each family resided in their own home and meals were consumed there, although they were cooked in a central kitchen. Like the Amanas and Rappites, Zoarites had access to a communal store where each family had an account. Until 1845, children resided in a communal children's house, then due to pressure from parents, the children left the collective housing provided by the community and returned to their parents' homes. By 1898, Zoar had lost most of its young people and as was common among many of the religious based groups, the young people were not as committed to the religious beliefs as their grandparents and parents. The property was divided among the remaining members and the history of another communal utopia was written (Oved, 1993, p. 82).

The Mormons have experimented with communalism, in a variety of forms, since the early 1830s. Joseph Smith, the founder of the Mormons, first introduced communalism via an economic program called the Law of Consecration and Stewardship. Brigham Young, a successor of Smith, tried again in the 1870s and 1880s to implement economic communalism known as the United Order movement. Smith believed that economic communalism and celestial or plural marriage, otherwise known as polygamy, were important steps in preparing for the millennium. Both of these practices were not looked upon favorably by the government (Altman & Ginat, 1996; May, 1997, p. 136).

Neither the Law of Consecration and Stewardship or the United Order movement were fully implemented or universally followed by all Mormons. Early Mormonism was concerned with fostering family and societal unity and Joseph Smith began to build the city of Zion in Missouri during 1831 to 1833 to fulfill an Old Testament prophecy. Consecration and Stewardship was practiced in Jackson County, Missouri, the site of Smith's new city of Zion. Families built and were responsible for their own homes. The Mormons were forced out of Missouri by non-Mormons and relocated to Nauvoo, Illinois where they were eventually forced to leave before settling in what was to become Utah. Some 200 United Order movements had been organized by 1874, but the vast majority never became fully operational. Orderville was one of the more successful United Order developments begun in 1875. Members ate together in a communal dining hall, lived in apartments, and wore uniforms. An elected board supervised all activity (dePillis, 1985, p. 39; May, 1997, p. 139).

Polygamy was a repressive system, but at the same time Mormon women had more options available to them than their female contemporaries. Mormons believed that the primary goal of marriage was to have children and raise them up to be righteous individuals. They argued that polygamy allowed the best men to have an abundance of children and they did not think that polygamy was demeaning to women (Foster, 1981, 1991; Kern, 1981; Muncy, 1973). Although Mormons no longer practice polygamy, there are numerous Mormon sects (not affiliated with the Church of Jesus Christ of Latter-day Saints) in the western United States that continue to practice polygamy and a modified form of communalism (Altman & Ginat, 1996; Kephart & Zellner, 1994, p. 269).

Five Icarian communities were constructed in the United States by the followers of French political radical Etienne Cabet. The term Icarian came from a book Cabet had published in 1839 where he described a utopia without money and private property. The two best-known communities were in Nauvoo, Illinois and Corning, Iowa. Nauvoo was formerly inhabited by the Mormons, who left when their leader Joseph Smith was murdered. The Mormons sold their property to the Icarians in 1849 (Sutton, 1997, p. 279).

Their communities were based on equality and each family was given two rooms in an apartment building. When children reached the age of four they became wards of the society and lived at a community boarding school. All meals were taken in a common dining room and all adults were assigned some type of work in one of the communal enterprises. Marriage was an integral component of life and celibacy was frowned upon. They did not practice a religion, but they were expected to be ethical in their dealings with one another. Once the Icarians moved to Iowa, families lived in their own homes. By 1898, the Icarian movement ended due in part to economic issues, resistance to change their constitution, and the departure of many young people (Sutton, 1997, p. 283).

Frenchman Charles Fourier was a utopian visionary who designed what were to become planned cooperative communities called phalanxes. Fourier lamented the evils of capitalism and the competitiveness which it engendered. His phalanxes would be located in the country and would include a massive central building or phalanstery which would contain apartments, a dining facility, communal rooms, galleries, etc. Across from the phalanstery would be workshops and warehouses surrounded by gardens, orchards, and forests (Guarneri, 1997, p. 160).

The Fourierist Phalanxes were identified as examples of utopian socialism and communitarian socialism. They were not religious sects or groups like many of their utopian counterparts of the day. They truly embraced communalism from the start and they intended, by their example, to sway all of society to this lifestyle. The Phalanxes were conservative regarding sexual and family matters. The traditional nuclear family was dominant and children were raised by their parents. Sex roles were typical of what one would find in nineteenth-century America. Over two dozen Phalanxes were undertaken, with nearly 15,000 participants. The last Fourierist experiment in the United States ended in 1892 (Guarneri, 1997, p. 169).

What attributed to the demise of the Phalanxes? More than anything, the participants were idealists and as Berry (1992, p. 91) states, "They lacked the focused commitment to goals that made the more disciplined religious experiments work."

Robert Owen was a wealthy industrialist from Scotland who, like Charles Fourier, was appalled with capitalism and its effects on the lives of working people. Owenism influenced the development of 29 communities, 19 of them in the United States, primarily during the 1820s and 1840s. Owen purchased the former Rappite property in New Harmony, Indiana in 1825 (Pitzer, 1997b, p. 122). Owen rejected religion, believed the nuclear family should be replaced by a community of families, and advocated the dissolution of traditional marriage. While New Harmony idealized equality of the sexes, women often found themselves regulated to the traditional domestic roles. This created tension in New Harmony and other Owenite communities which eventually lead to their demise. Women were never truly accepted as equals (Oved, 1993, p. 58).

The French, German, and British were not the only ones interested in creating utopias in the United States. Another Pietist group, driven from Europe by the Lutherans, were the Swedish Janssonists. Eric Jansson, the leader of the Janssonists, considered himself the second incarnation of Jesus Christ. Most of the Janssonists immigrated to the United States between 1846 and 1854. In July of 1846, Jansson and his followers arrived in Illinois and started what came to be known as the Bishop Hill Colony. They practiced community of goods and in the years from 1846 to 1848 practiced celibacy and discouraged marriages, but in 1848 the community began to prosper and the rule on celibacy was lifted. Over 50 couples married during the summer of 1848 (Wagner, 1997, p. 304).

Nuclear families resided in single rooms within communal dwellings, which also contained communal dining rooms. The division of labor followed along traditional gender lines. By 1850, Bishop Hill was a successful communal undertaking, its farm was productive and the community was thriving. By 1861, the community had dissolved due, in part, to poor investing of colony money (Wagner, 1997, p. 310).

The Hutterites

The Hutterites, also known as the Hutterian Brethren or Brethren, are an Anabaptist religious group who trace their beginning to the Swiss Anabaptist movement in Zurich, Switzerland in 1525. They were viewed as heretics by Catholics and Protestants. Jakob Hutter emerged as a radical Anabaptist leader who preached against infant baptism and warfare, while supporting community of goods (Gutergemeinschaft) and the separation of church and state. Self-surrender or submission to the will of God and the community (Gelassenheit) became a key element of early Hutterite communitarianism and continues to be an important characteristic of Hutterite identity today (Oved, 1993, p. 335). Although Hutter eventually became leader of what was to become the Hutterites, the group was actually formed in 1528 by a dissentient group of Anabaptists who fled to Moravia, which is now the country of Czechoslovakia. Hutter arrived in 1529, with his own group, and by 1533 assumed control of the Anabaptists, reinstating the biblically based principle of communalism. The Hutterites have experienced three periods of community of goods: 1528 to 1695, 1763 to 1818, and 1859 to present (Kephart, 1982).

The Hutterites, as well as other Anabaptist groups, experienced a history of persecution at the hands of Protestant and Catholic leaders. The Hutterites left Moravia and fled to Transylvania and Slovakia, eventually leaving in 1770 to settle in the Ukraine. The Russian government promised them they could live communally, openly, and freely, practice their religion, and be free from military service. By 1870, the Russian government became less tolerant of the Hutterites and demanded that they serve in the military. The Hutterites could not abide by this change and began to search for a new homeland which brought them to North America beginning in 1874 (Kephart, 1982).

Between 1874 and 1879, 1,200 members emigrated from Russia to the United States the majority of whom had not been living communally in Russia. Three groups of Hutterites, the Schmiedeleut, the Dariusleut, and the Lehrerleut, practiced community of goods, while a fourth group known as the Prairieleut chose not to live communally with the others and purchased pre-existing farms or acquired land through the Homestead Act of 1862 (Janzen 1994). By 1880, there were 443 Hutterites who were practicing community of goods. The first Schmiedeleut colony (Bon Homme) was started in 1874, followed by a Dariusleut colony (Wolf Creek) in 1875, and a Lehrerleut colony (Elmspring) in1877. These three colonies have grown to almost 400 colonies (two thirds in western Canada and the remaining one third in South Dakota, North Dakota, Montana, Washington, and Minnesota) with approximately

36,000 members making the Hutterites one of the largest communal organizations in the world (Huntington, 1997, p. 334).

The Hutterites prospered in America from their arrival in 1874 until 1917. The Selective Service Act of 1917 mandated that even conscientious objectors, such as the Hutterites, would have to serve in some capacity in the armed forces. Two young Hutterite men died in 1918 at Fort Leavenworth, Kansas, from injuries they sustained while interned in a variety of prisons for refusing to wear the military uniform. All but the Bon Homme colony relocated to Canada, 15 colonies had settled in Canada by 1918. Some of the Hutterites eventually returned to the United States during the 1930s because of some changes in the law which they found favorable. Also life in Canada was not as tranquil as they had hoped for. Some Canadians were antipacifists and anti-German and by the early 1940s land restriction laws were implemented which temporarily limited Hutterite expansion (Oved, 1993, p. 354; Berry, 1992, p. 123).

The Hutterites are often confused with their Anabaptist cousins the Mennonites and Amish. The major difference between these three groups is that the Hutterites live communally (Smith, 1996b). Another group, often mistaken for the Hutterites, is the Society of Brothers (the Bruderhof or sometimes known as the Hutterian Society of Brothers) (Zablocki, 1971). This group was once affiliated with the Hutterites, but in 1990 the Dariusleut and the Lehrerleut Hutterites terminated their relationship with the Society of Brothers as did the Schmiedeleut in 1996 (Huntington, 1997, p. 336).

Each Hutterite colony is guided by an elected council consisting of five to seven baptized men. The council is headed by the first preacher and the other men tend to be those who hold important positions in the colony such as the German school teacher, the field manager, the second preacher, and the colony steward. The preachers are elected by lot with no formal education for the position. Hutterite society is patriarchal and traditional regarding sex roles and the division of labor. Women are viewed as being inferior both intellectually and physically to men. Women are usually relegated to domestic chores such as cleaning, child care, and food preparation, while men do most of the farming and income-producing work (Hostetler, 1977).

Hutterite colonies are large agricultural enterprises that consist of 100 to 150 members. When the community population reaches 130, plans are begun to create a new colony by splitting the present one in half. The Hutterites farm thousands of acres; many colonies own and/or lease up to 25,000 acres of land. A study conducted in the 1988 revealed that on the average, a Montana Hutterite colony owned 10,162 acres and leased an additional 3,602 acres (Smith, 1991, p. 66). The Hutterites also raise livestock and fowl for their own consumption and for sale. They use the latest technology to remain economically competitive, such as computers and automated farm machinery, although they are selective about what aspects of modernity they allow in their apartments and other noneconomic areas of the colony. Family life is an integral component of community life in a Hutterite colony, the major function of the family is to have children and take care of them until the colony assumes responsibility for them. The Hutterites believe it is the responsibility of the everyone in the colony, not just the biological parents, to socialize individuals especially children and young adults (Hostetler, 1977, p. 203). Hutterite socialization is a continuous process with two key moments, baptism as an adult and death (Hostetler & Huntington, 1996, p. 63).

Hutterite families live in buildings that contain four families, each with their own apartments. There are two bedrooms and an all-purpose living room in each apartment. As a family grows, they can request more rooms. Meals are eaten in the colony dining room, although snacks are allowed in the apartments. Each colony has a communal laundry and bath house. There is little privacy in Hutterite life, especially in the apartments where it is common for people to walk in and out without knocking (Hostetler, 1977, p. 203).

Kinship in Hutterite society is patrilineal and patrilocal, while females usually marry outside their colony but within their Hutterite federation or leut. The average age of marriage for men is 26 and for women it is 25; few persons remain single and divorce is virtually nonexistent. Hutterite men and women must be baptized before they can marry. Average family size varies from colony to colony, but within a range of five to seven family members. Fertility rates have been declining for several decades, although the Hutterites do not use birth control. The Hutterites have maintained the extended family and it is not uncommon for three to four generations to reside in the same colony. Another common occurrence is for a colony to have only one family name, but there might be eight to fourteen extended families within the same colony. This is due to the high degree of intermarriage and frequently it is the source of tension within the colony. Family factions often form power blocks resulting in some families being excluded from status positions, and as Karl Peter (1987, p. xxii) states, "Hutterites like to portray themselves as "saintly" people . . . Hutterites are no more saintly or unsaintly than other sectarian groups."

Children spend their first 3 years at home then when they turn 3 they are enrolled in the colony kindergarten. At 6 years of age they transfer to the regular school where they are instructed by the German teacher and the English teacher. Children stay there until they are 15 when they can be integrated into the colony labor force. It is the child's experience in the kindergarten which signals to them the need to conform to the norms of the colony. They become keenly aware that the community is put first and individuals second (Peter, 1987, p. 62).

Marriage brings more changes for women than men. Wives have to relocate to their husband's colony and become acquainted with a new peer group away from their own families. While a husband remains in his colony, he must shift his identification to the group of young married men instead of the group of young unmarried men. With marriage comes more responsible positions in the occupational hierarchy. The husband-wife relationship is defined by its connection with the overall communal structure.

Work separates the couple for the major portion of the day into same-sex groups and even their meals are eaten with their respective sex group. Newlyweds are often assigned a bedroom across from their parents, but usually within a year they move to another building (Peter, 1987, p. 77).

As we have done with the Shakers and the Oneida Community, let us apply Kanter's theory of commitment to the Hutterites. They live an austere lifestyle which is one form of sacrifice, and while their income (communal income, Hutterites do not draw salaries) is substantially more than most farming families, much of it is used for the building of new colonies. Although individual Hutterites do not have property or assets to invest in the colony, they do invest their total lives in the community. For most Hutterites, life outside the colony is not an alternative for them. Renunciation is a powerful mechanism which reinforces the belief that Hutterite life is the only way to achieve salvation. Maintaining boundaries between the Hutterites and the outside world strengthens their identity. While the family is more important among the Hutterites than it was among the Shakers and the Oneida Community, children learn that the community is more important than the family, and as S. C. Lee and Audrey Brattrud (1967, p. 513) found, the colony acts as an extended family and therefore the nuclear family does not function as a primary group. The mechanism of Communion is fully integrated into the everyday life of Hutterite society. Shared property, communal work, communal dining and worship services, among other indicators builds commitment within the colony. Through mortification and the socialization process Hutterites learn to submit to the will of community rather than their own will (Gelassenheit). Transcendence fully permeates Hutterite life. Their lives are directed toward attaining eternal life and they lead their lives according to biblical precepts (Hassinger & Pinkerton, 1986, p. 397).

Family Versus Community: A Synopsis

Because of space limitations, we have only looked at a handful of historic communal utopias. The groups we have studied so far were selected because of their notoriety and for their handling of the nuclear family. Several points can be drawn from them. The first half of the nineteenth century, in Europe and the United States, was a time of great economic, political, and social change. Connected to these changes, in unique ways, was the institution of religion. As we have noted many of these groups, especially the Pietist sects, but also the Shakers and the Hutterites, were and are millennialists. They blended communalism together with their religious ideology. Most, but not all, of the religious groups endorsed the practice of celibacy, at one time or another, in the life of their communities.

Although most communal utopias had policies regarding family life, nuclear families survived whether as single units or as members of a large communal family. Those that maintained nuclear families, such as Amana, the Rappites, and the Hutterites, created a system where the families were dependent on the community for their survival and well-being. The use of the community store and other services provided by the community allowed the group to exert some control over and reduce the autonomy of nuclear families. Attempts were made to dissolve traditional families, two examples are the Shakers and the Oneida Community. The Shakers were successful in altering traditional family life, but that eventually has led to the near extinction of that community. The Oneidans eventually dissolved their complex marriage system and returned to traditional monogamous marriage. The leaders of Amana were astute enough to realize that long-time survival was linked to a controlled nuclear family situation.

We have also seen that although equality between the sexes was a goal of some of these communal utopias, few truly attained that goal. The Shakers and Oneida made progress in this area, while the Hutterites make no attempt to work toward equality between the sexes. In addition, regarding marriage, family, and gender role issues, it appears that economics played a very important role in the survival and failure of these communal utopias.

Alongside the role economics played in the survival of these groups, another important factor, which contributed to the demise of historic communal utopias, was the difficulty they had in socializing their young with the idealism of the founders of their groups. Another factor that helps to explain the demise of these groups is that maintaining a gemeinschaft way of life was a constant struggle for them especially in a country and world which was infected with the spirit of modernity. The saying, you can run but you can not hide, is as true today as it was back in the nineteenth century. Gesellschaft ideas infiltrated the boundaries of these communities and changed them forever.

Success is a difficult issue to assess as Jon Wagner (1985) discusses in his influential article and it should be viewed multidimensionally rather than unidimensionally. He identified the following seven criteria of communal success: achievement of its own goals, attains some degree of social perfection, longevity, size, degree of social cohesion, has influenced society, and provides for the personal growth of its members.

Longevity, although an important indicator of success or failure, by itself, tells us little about the accomplishments of communal groups. Communal utopias disintegrate and eventually fail for a variety of reasons, not necessarily ones related to family life. Stagnation and assimilation are two potential disintegration processes which are determined by the distinct characteristics of individual communes (Niv, 1980, p. 383).

Developmental Communalism is an approach which broadens our analysis of communal success by examining how communal groups evolved over time, even when communal living had been abandoned (Pitzer, 1997, p. 137). The developmental communalism approach includes criteria discussed by Wagner (1985). Communal history should be viewed through the lenses of this approach.

How one applies these and other criteria will determine to what degree the community, in question, is successful. The communal utopias we have investigated in Chapters 3 and 4 were all viewed as successful, although they varied by type of ideology, the use of commitment mechanisms, and duration.

Conclusion

Several of the historic communal utopias discussed in this chapter had their roots in Europe. George Rapp broke from the Lutheran Church, in Germany, and immigrated with some of his followers to the United States. Five Icarian communities were built in the United States by followers of French political radical Etienne Cabet. Charles Fourier, a Frenchman, designed planned communities called phalanxes. Robert Owen, an industrialist from Scotland, was influential in the founding of nineteen communities. Eric Jansson and his followers emigrated from Sweden in the mid-1800s. The Hutterites, originally formed in Moravia, arrived in the United States from Russia in 1874.

As we saw with the Shakers, Oneida, and Amana, family life among the historic communal utopias discussed in the present chapter varied from group to group. Ephrata, the Rappites, Zoar, and the Janssonists practiced celibacy, although the Zoar and the Janssonists later lifted the rule of celibacy. The Mormons practiced polygamy, while the Icarians frowned upon celibacy and considered marriage as important. The Fourierist Phalanxes supported nuclear families, while Owenite communities attempted to replace nuclear families with communal families and dissolve traditional marriages. The Hutterites view the nuclear family as important, but subordinate to the colony.

In Chapter 5, we shift our focus to the latter part of the twentieth century and to a period of time when communal living and nontraditional families gained the attention of the media and the American public. The 1960s and 1970s were decades when the United States experienced a great degree of social change regarding values and behaviors. The countercultural movement, the civil rights movement, the anti-Vietnam War movement, and the feminist movement were prominent social movements which contributed to the turbulence of the times and pressed Americans to reevaluate the status quo and their own value systems. For some, the urban and rural communes of the 1960s and 1970s were an escape, for others they were a place for a new beginning.

We must also realize that communal activity was occurring throughout the latter decades of the nineteenth century and up through the first half of the twentieth century. Jewish agricultural colonies, Theosophical communities, Socialist and anarchistic utopias, and the Peace Mission movement, among others, occupied the years prior to the beginning of the most recent surge (1960 to present) in communal living in the United States.

5

Urban and Rural Communes of the 1960s and 1970s

The common belief in the media and among some scholars was that the onset of rural communes in the 1960s was primarily the result of the decay and fragmentation of urban hippie life in places like Haight-Ashbury, the East Village, and other urban enclaves. Miller (1992b, p. 74) argues in the following passage that new communes, especially rural ones, were appearing prior to the identification of a hippie culture in the United States.

> The hippies evolved from the beats of the 1950s and the bohemians of the decades before that, but it would be hard to see them as coalescing into anything that amounted to a distinct social movement before about 1966.

Although some communes were founded by hippies who left urban enclaves, communal living as an alternative lifestyle has a long history in the United States and it is not a new cultural phenomenon (Miller, 1992b, p. 74). Our previous discussion of historic communal utopias in Chapter 3 is evidence supporting this most important point. Miller (1992b, p. 75) states, "In short, the communes were more closely related to the tradition of cultural dissent than they were to the breakdown of the hip urban centers." The hippies were not inventing some new lifestyle, instead they were creating a late twentieth century version of communal living.

Without the tradition of American cultural radicalism, the communal movement of the 1960s would not have developed as it did (Veysey, 1978, p. 456). Mysticism and anarchism, as in previous epochs, were two of the most visible trends of American cultural radicalism within the 1960s and 1970s communal movement (Veysey, 1978, p. 9). The success of rural and urban communes was determined, in large part, by the interplay of structure and charisma, which were defining elements of each trend. This will continue to be true for communes in the twenty-first century.

Rural communes were more serious communal living experiments than urban communes because they required participants to make a more deliberate choice (Berger, Hackett, & Millar, 1972, p. 419). Jerome (1974) and Gardner (1978) echo the sentiments of Berger et al. and argue that urban communes were less innovative and serious than rural communes, while Kanter and Halter (1973b) and Kanter (1979) dispute that position and Zablocki (1980, p. 45) found few differences between urban and rural communes. Urban communes were more numerous than rural communes and although they were less sectarian and frequently provided fewer services for their members, urban communes tended to be more flexible communities. As Zablocki (1980, p. 45) concludes they were, "The most significant response to alienation from contemporary society."

The alienation that Zablocki speaks of was very real and concrete, it was not abstract. As we discussed in Chapter 1, alienation, according to Nisbet (1966), is the outcome of the loss of community. The loss of community or gemeinschaft was the result of modernity and our society's changing value system and as Kephart (1987, p. 266) states, "It is not possible to understand the communal movement of 1965-1975 without having some awareness of the underlying social unrest that existed at the time."

Gardner (1978, p. 9) claims two youth movements combined to produce the surge in rural communes, "The drug-based hippie culture and the student-based political movement joined in a shared vision of the apocalypse." If there was one defining concept of the rural commune movement it was voluntary primitivism. Gardner (1978, p. 14) states,

> The essence of voluntary primitivism was a deliberate withdrawal from the institutions and structures of modern life and the voluntary acceptance of a reduced standard of living, both as a way out of a destructive and oppressive social system and as a positive, freedom-enhancing end in itself.

According to Kanter and Halter (1973b) and Kanter (1979), urban communes of the 1970s have little in common with rural communes. Urban communes of the 1960s, but particularly those of the early 1970s, were not retreats from society, nor were they attempting to create a new society. Kanter (1979, p. 112) argues, "Urban communes exist to create a collective household, a shared home, an augmented family."

Urban communes can be visualized as substitute families (Levine, Carr, and Horenblas, 1973, p. 162). When they function well they can be places of nurturance and love. The goals of urban communes are not mutually exclusive from those of families. One of the goals of urban communes was to redefine sex roles in family life. Rural communes as a whole maintained traditional sex roles, while urban communes attempted to rewrite the role scripts for men and women and enact the changes. Urban communes were appealing to young professionals, single parents, and middle-class families. Not everyone was equipped to live a rural "back to the land" lifestyle, a lesson most rural communalists learned the hard way and which eventually led to the failure of many, if not most of the communities and utopias they had hoped to construct.

Surprisingly, those modern communards studied by Zablocki (1980, p. 97), came from nuclear families where both parents were present, along with at least one sibling. Communalists, as a whole, came from loving and intimate family environments. I stated this was surprising because the common belief was that the young people who were flocking to communes were rebelling against the nuclear family. Communitarianism flourishes "among those who came from tight-knit nuclear families" not from "among those with traumatic experiences in early life."

The ability to trust, which is characteristically developed in healthy families, is an essential ingredient for successful communes. The most common reasons given for joining a communal household were ideological, relational, personal, and for convenience (Zablocki, 1980, p. 105). While the communalists came from primarily privileged and intact nuclear families, they also held an idealized vision of social life. This vision was a utopian one, predicated on the beliefs of human perfectibility, order, brotherhood, the union of mind and body, experimentation, and coherence as a group. These beliefs are linked by their concern with harmony. Historic utopians and modern communards are connected by their belief that one becomes fully human only in collective situations. Communal living brings order out of chaos (Kanter, 1972).

Two branches developed within the communal movement of the 1960s and 1970s: a counter culture and an alternate culture (Conover, 1978, p. 8). Although these two branches were often viewed as one, there were distinctions between them. An alternate culture focused on creating a new world by example, while a counter culture attempted to change the existing world through politics and even revolution. Alternate cultures were more concerned with achieving their ends or goals of restoring gemeinschaft, while the counter cultures focused on the means of change (reforming society) rather than creating a new one. By far, the majority of communal utopias were alternate cultures, not counter cultures. Most modern counter cultures dissolved in the late 1960s because the revolution failed. They either disbanded or reconstituted themselves into alternate cultures, better known as alternative communities. The communal movement peaked in the late 1960s and early 1970s and gradually receded as the novelty of the movement and the times changed. An issue which plagued both rural and urban communes was the dilemma between personal freedom and communal obligations, as we discussed in the first section of Chapter 1. Gardner (1978, p. 245) reached an intriguing conclusion based on his study of rural communes, communal sharing was not related to group survival, as one would surmise, and when it was present to a large degree, it shortened the longevity of the commune. Basically the only resources rural communalists shared were land and the buildings on the property (Gardner, 1978, p. 229). Inevitably, members of extended-family communes (often referred to as urban communes) found that they too did not have the energy to create an alternative life where sharing played such a high-profile role (Ruth, 1978, p. 76). These findings should not be surprising considering the communalists were reared and socialized in gesellschaft environments that rewarded individualism, not collective undertakings.

The Status of Families in Rural and Urban Communes

Some, but not all, of the communes in the 1960s and 1970s desired to construct family-like settings where warmth and intimacy prevailed. Kanter (1973a, p. 401) states,

> While communes seek to become families, they are, at the same time, something different from families; they are groups with their own unique form, something between communities, organizations, families, and friendship groups, and they contain families in their midst as well as generate family-like feeling throughout the whole communal group.

We also know from the work done by Aidala (1983) and Zablocki (1980) that communalists talked about family-oriented topics, but few communes were actually focused on the family or wanted to create families. As we discussed in Chapter 1, the vast majority of communalists during the 1960s and 1970s were temporarily dropping out of mainstream society and seeking companionship among like-minded individuals. Although as Zablocki (1980, p. 202) reminds us, even though most did not join communes to specifically create families, they were not necessarily against working at intimacy and emotional security.

With these points in mind, it is difficult to speak authoritatively and universally about family life in modern communes. Family life, however it was defined, was a mixed bag of roles and behaviors that varied from place to place. Keep in mind that there were thousands of communes during this time, based on a wide range of ideologies. Even when groups claimed to be families, that was no guarantee they were. Kanter (1973a; 1977; 1979) and Kanter and Halter (1973b) are much more adamant in claiming that urban communalists were serious about building families than Aidala (1983; 1989) and Aidala and Zablocki (1991). The various data sets have led these researchers to different conclusions about family life in the communal utopias of the 1960s and 1970s. Let us now look at several examples of groups that existed during this era and how they dealt with familial issues.

The Ranch, a rural California commune, was noncreedal and anarchist. Berger (1981, p. 29) describes it as "a post-hippie 'family' commune." The Ranch would fit Kanter's (1972) classification of a retreat commune. The major undertaking of The Ranch was to create a family. The Ranch consisted of 140 acres of land where approximately 24 adults and their children resided in their own homes. Meals were shared in the communal dining room and there was a communal outhouse. They lived without electricity and telephones, but used kerosene lamps for light and wood for heat and cooking. Most of their food was home grown in gardens and a greenhouse, plus they had goats, chickens, and geese. Natural childbirth was common and it was a joyous event for the whole commune. Although The Ranch was not sexist and ideologically supported equality, there was a tendency toward a traditional division of labor and sex roles, this was not uncommon among rural communes even those espousing equality like The Ranch. The women's movement did have an impact in the mid-1970s and women became less reliant on men. Children were viewed just like everyone else in the commune and men appeared to be more involved in the childrens' lives than men in other settings. Children were supervised not just by their parents, but by all adults in the commune. Children were given much more freedom to experiment with drugs and sex than one would find in other communes.

The Ranch established their own school which enhanced relationships between members and fueled their image of family. Many of the members told Berger (1981, p. 96) that their family lives as children were lacking and they intended to do things differently than their parents did. Members were expected to love each other and sexual exclusiveness was frowned upon even among those who were couples. Intimate sexual relationships were encouraged as long as both members found them rewarding. Berger found couples tended to not be continuously together while they resided at The Ranch. The Ranch was not a group marriage (also known as multilateral marriage, which is a situation where "three or more partners, each of whom considers himself/herself to be married or committed . . . to more than one of the other partners") (Constantine & Constantine, 1973, p. 49), it began as an intentional extended family consisting of nuclear families, but they did experiment sexually. Berger (1981, p. 133) comments that it is not surprising that people who live and work together would develop sexual attractions for one another. Even though they considered themselves a family, their definition of family did not include an incest taboo. Some members left when they realized they wanted more of a nuclear family emphasis; singles often found it difficult to blend in with the group especially if they were involved with someone outside of the commune.

In rural communes, family is community; the closeness of living quarters and the density of interaction make it objectively difficult to dissemble; people's lives are more or less fully exposed to their brothers and sisters, and any attempt to disguise feelings or emotions is likely to be vain and therefore disapproved (why bother?). (Berger, 1981, p. 159)

The previous quote is very revealing, not just for The Ranch, but for communes in general. Over time, your fellow members can determine whether your intentions are genuine or not and they can determine one's level of commitment to the group. Let us now apply Kanter's commitment mechanisms to The Ranch. The most noticeable dimension of sacrifice at The Ranch is the reduced standard of living the members experience in comparison to their prior urban middle-class existence. They make do with fewer material possessions in their rural communal life. Investment is not required for membership and it appears to play a minimal role in the life of the communalists. Relinquishing one's membership is not viewed as a great cost to the individual. Of all the mechanisms, renunciation is the most important one at The Ranch. Physical isolation from the outside world forms the ideological basis of The Ranch and this element of renunciation also enhances their goal of self-sufficiency. Because The Ranch acts as an extended family, communion is an important mechanism for them. Shared work, meals, living in common, and striving to promote and enact communal ideas enhances the role communion plays in the commitment building process at The Ranch. Mortification is not used by members to any great extent, although personal pretensions appear to be kept in check. Transcendence is not a major factor for this group; they have no plan for improving society nor do they have any great concerns for the hereafter (Hassinger & Pinkerton, 1986, p. 405).

The Farm was established in 1971 in Tennessee by its charismatic leader Stephen Gaskin and 1,000 other middle-class college students from San Francisco. Presently, there are 250 residents. The Farm is a rural, mystical communal utopia and, according to Kanter's (1972) classification, would be identified as a service commune. The Farm is very structured in contrast to The Ranch.

Families are very important parts of the community at The Farm. Marriage is held in high esteem and viewed as an essential ingredient for a happy life. Promiscuity, including premarital sex and adultery, is not allowed. The same is true for artificial birth control. The Farm has a rigid sexual division of labor based in part on patterns found in the traditional American family and therefore they have been accused of maintaining sexual inequality because of their differentiated sex-role system. They expect women to cook and clean, but they do not allow men to be promiscuous, aggressive, or dominant. They have tried group marriage, but have returned to monogamous relationships. The Farm, according to Bryan Pfaffenberger (1982, p. 174), has done exactly what communal scholars (Conover, 1972; Kanter, 1972; Ramey, 1972) indicate they should not do if they want to succeed and Pfaffenberger claims that, "The Farm, then, is truly enigmatic." Then again, the Hutterites have done the same thing and they have successful colonies. One reason for the success of The Farm and the Hutterites, and as we will see in the next chapter with Jesus People USA, is their respective religious ideology. Religious communes, in comparison to secular or noncreedal communes, tend to be more successful.

Families live in their own homes and the community has its own school. They are strict vegetarians and grow most of their food. Members want to create an alternative society based on spiritual qualities linking Hinduism, Buddhism, Zen, Christianity, and humanistic psychology. They shun materialism and they are involved in community outreach programs.

Part of their success is attributed to the attention they give to developing small groups. A permanent marriage is viewed as the nucleus of these small groups which create close households or families of up to 30 people. They consider themselves to be living in a family monastery. They believe that marriages can be enhanced if the partners are willing to submit themselves to joining these small families or households where they will be among critical, yet compassionate members (Pfaffenberger, 1982, p. 201). Let us now apply Kanter's (1972) theory of commitment to The Farm.

Sacrifice is used to build commitment to the group through rejecting the materialism of modern American society and by adhering to a strict vegetarian diet. Members are expected to turn over all of their material goods once they have been accepted for membership and they are expected to work in the communal enterprises, thus investment is an integral mechanism for The Farm. The Farm's physical isolation enhances members' ability to renounce the outside world. Shared work enhances a feeling of communion and builds relationships among members. Mortification is not used much at The Farm, although the community is expected to be placed above the individual. The most important mechanism for The Farm is transcendence and this is fostered through the religious beliefs of the group and the charisma of Gaskin (Hassinger & Pinkerton, 1986, p. 407).

Of the 120 rural and urban communes studied by Zablocki (1980), 6 rural and 9 urban communes or 9% of his sample were alternative families (either patriarchal, matriarchal, fraternal, or group marriage). Let us now look briefly at the three alternative family communes discussed by Zablocki in his book *Alienation and Charisma*.

White Tower was a patriarchal (there was a charismatic leader) urban commune whose primary goal was to create an extended family. Adults treated each other as brother and sister and functioned as parents to all the children. They experimented sexually with swapping partners and they were egalitarian and strove for group consensus (Zablocki, 1980, p. 227).

Earth Mother was a matriarchal rural commune. Monogamy was the stated norm, but members did change mates frequently. Children were the responsibility of the commune not their parents and women wielded power primarily because they exhibited greater commitment to the commune and longevity of membership. The group demanded commitment to the commune, but also fostered personal freedom. This position was a constant source of friction in the community (Zablocki, 1980, p. 228).

The Family was a group marriage rural commune where child rearing and sex were shared. All adults were responsible for the children and it was expected that all adults would have sex with as many partners as possible. The sexual connection was viewed as their primary source of commitment. They were egalitarian regarding sex roles and the division of labor and the commune was anarchistic (Zablocki, 1980, p. 229).

While families were certainly present either as individual nuclear families or as communal families in the other communes Zablocki studied, those who were labeled as alternative family specifically identified themselves as families. Research conducted by Aidala (1989, p. 318) found that although commune members thought changes were needed in conventional marriage and parenting practices they did not reject either. They were rather ambivalent and uncertain about what changes should be made among the conventional choices available to them. For example, a slight majority believed it was healthier for children to be raised in a commune than a nuclear family, although one third of them were uncertain. One third of them were positive about singlehood, while 35% were uncertain.

Kshama Ferrar (1982, p. 10) examined 42 families from 22 communes who participated in Zablocki's (1980) study. Parents residing in communes which accommodated family needs were more satisfied with communal life, than parents who resided in communes where family needs were incidental to the focus of the commune. Parents from multiple family households frequently experienced conflict over child rearing, while parents from isolated family households found it difficult to maintain a balance between family needs and the needs of the commune. Ferrar (1982, p. 12) found that the majority of parents who are ex-members cited among their reasons for leaving dissatisfaction with the child rearing situation in their commune.

Families in isolated central households were more satisfied than families in multiple central households, while families in multiple incidental households were more satisfied than families in isolated incidental households. In response to the question, "How do you feel about this commune as a place to raise your children?" isolated central families stated their households were excellent places to raise children. Multiple central families indicated very good to excellent, multiple incidental families replied very good, and isolated incidental families responded their households were good places to rear children (Ferrar, 1982, p. 12).

During 1971 to 1978, Noreen Cornfield (1983) studied 32 secular urban communes in Chicago. The study focused on identifying conditions which led to the success of communal life, which was calculated by members' satisfaction and the duration of the commune. While Cornfield did not specifically address the issue of whether or not these communes were families, she did use variables related to family life. Economic prudence, prior acquaintance of members, housework is regularly done, parental responsibilities, voluntary time limitation, and amount of private time were elements of conventionality or conventional behavior. Nonexclusive sexual relations, property sharing, and high involvement in the commune were elements of unconventional behavior.

All of the elements of conventionality except prior acquaintance of members and parental responsibilities enhanced satisfaction, while duration was increased by all of the elements of conventionality except voluntary time limitation and regular housework. One nonconventional element, high communal involvement, increased duration. This is an interesting finding considering what Gardner (1978) found in his study of rural communes. Property sharing and nonmonogamy, both unconventional behaviors, had no direct effects on success (Cornfield, 1983, p. 115). Cornfield found that although communal households identify themselves as alternative communities, conventional behaviors are a necessary ingredient for their success.

Middle-class communes are essentially extended families and Sterling Alam (1978, p. 86) questions how appropriate is it to consider them an alternative family form. He uses a similar method as Cornfield by employing the use of conventional and nonconventional family norms. He states that middle-class communes lie somewhere in between a total acceptance or a total rejection of conventional family norms. The following are elements of conventionality describing the ideal type of conventional family: obligatory, nuclear, patriarchal, permanent, legalized, role differentiated, emotional, economic, sexual, monogamous, neolocal, exclusive, procreative, and parental. He acknowledges that extended family communes would reject the first six elements or characteristics and therefore he considers this enough of a rejection of the conventional family to be considered an alternative family form.

Jon Wagner (1982b, p. 33) identifies an important point which impacts our discussion of family life in modern communes. He rightly concludes, that there are differences between corporate and noncorporate communal societies and the family dynamics which occur within each type. Larger communes, those with over 20 members, usually have formal structures and ideologies with clearly defined goals and frequently there are charismatic leaders too, while smaller communes tend to have informal structures and ideologies.

Larger communes have, according to Wagner (1982b, p. 33),

> An identity and a set of purposes to which the newcomer must adapt and which can survive independently of the comings and goings of particular members. Such a commune has a "corpus" which transcends its individual parts (members), hence the term "corporate." Corporate communes stand in contrast to the small "family" communes. In the latter, all ideologies and structures are negotiable and held answerable to the felt needs of individual members, whose participation defines the group rather than vice versa.

There are major differences between corporate and noncorporate communes particularly regarding sex roles. While the evidence is fairly strong supporting the conclusion that in family communes there is a tendency toward equality, the same can not be said for contemporary corporate communes. The differences between these types of communes regarding sex roles is deeply rooted in the ideology of the group, whether the group recognizes there are sex-role conflicts, and if the conflicts are recognized what diagnosis or solution is found.

Communal maintenance also dictates the level and type of sex-role conflicts. Very rigid and structured communes tend to also be the largest and wealthiest communal utopias. Boundaries can be maintained, according to Wagner (1982b, p. 40), through either nonsexist means such as those practiced by the egalitarian group Twin Oaks (which will be discussed in the next chapter) or sexist ones such as patriarchy.

Urban communes promote change primarily through changing sex-role orientations and behaviors in the areas of the division of labor and emotional characteristics (Kanter & Halter, 1973b, p. 215). Urban communes on the whole, are smaller and thus more adaptive to these changes. They attribute the sex role changes primarily to ideological and structural conditions in these urban households. They admit that these changes are also influenced by a self-selection process of who is attracted to this lifestyle and therefore is amenable to the changing norms and roles (Kanter & Halter, 1973b, p. 198).

In their study of urban communes, Kanter and Halter (1973b, p. 198) found changes that were bringing about equal participation by men and women in domestic/household duties, a reduction in sex-related differences such as nurturance, support, and emotional expressiveness, and an opening and sharing of access to power and influence. All of these changes challenged the traditional system of sex roles operating in mainstream society as well as in many of what Wagner (1982b) calls "corporate" communes. More than anything, these urban communes were attempting to break down sex-role stereotypes and they were successful to some extent in broadening what was viewed as normative for both men and women. Even with all of these changes, child rearing still remained the responsibility of mothers.

Urban communes tended to be small and family-like and essentially the people within them were doing what individual nuclear families have done (Kanter & Halter, 1973b). These communes were less like rural or spiritual communes and more like extended families. Leigh Minturn (1984, p. 73) reached a similar conclusion that the sex roles of people living in communes evolve and become similar to those of persons in extended families. These urban communes were family alternatives which influenced society primarily through the interactions and behaviors of members within the household (Kanter & Halter, 1973b, p. 200).

The following statement by Kanter and Halter (1973b, p. 206) is revealing, "Thus, communes are no more interested in the strong, silent, power-hungry male stereotype than they are in the passive, helpless, whining female stereotype." People who emulated these stereotypes would be very destructive in urban communes and reduce, if not destroy, the goals of the commune. The researchers found that the stereotypes dissolved because of the type of people who joined these communes and the requirements or norms of their shared life. Those emulating the traditional stereotypes would not feel comfortable, nor accepted in these urban communes.

The role of urban communes as norm-changers is highlighted by Kanter and Halter (1973b, p. 216),

Perhaps most revolutionary is the fact that through communal living single people can participate in family life—the need to marry solely for intimate ties and family-like companionship may be virtually destroyed. The new urban domestic communes also offer something to the society, for they may be one of the last repositories of traditional American family virtues and values. In an era when more and more household and family functions are performed outside the home (including intimacy and companionship, for which we now have a wide range of secondary institutions), urban communes are trying to make these activities the center of a new kind of home.

As we read and reflect on this quote, some 25 years or more after it was written, it is rather obvious that urban communes have not replaced nuclear families. Likewise, when cohabitation became more visible and openly discussed in the late 1960s, the fear among conservatives was that if that trend continued it would eventually replace marriage. Although we know more people cohabit now then ever before, it has not replaced marriage and family life. Neither of these alternatives to traditional family life have become substitutes for it.

Urban communes did not pose any threat to family life, even if they became widespread and successful (Levine, Carr, & Horenblas, 1973, p. 162). In fact, they found them to be useful for identifying trouble spots in our society. These researchers anticipated changes in family life for some based on what our society was learning from these nontraditional families, but most importantly they indicated the message emanating from urban communes was that we need each other—sharing one's self with others has been at the foundation of communal life from the very beginning.

In Chapter 1, Popenoe's (1993b) definition was inclusive enough to include communes as families, but Kanter and Halter's claim that urban communes were "one of the last repositories of traditional American family virtues and values" might engender a debate with the various "family values" contingents who vie with each other for political and moral power. From a sociological point of view, Kanter and Halter were correct in their conclusion regarding the loss of family functions such as intimacy and companionship, among other functions by the way. Whether urban communes accomplished what Kanter and Halter claim they did in maintaining family virtues and values is a matter that needs more research.

Aidala's (1989, p. 311) follow-up study on urban communalists of the 1970s did find some support for the claims made by Kanter and Halter. Love and intimacy as personal values were still ranked high by her respondents, while ex-commune members are less likely to have married and many still live in multi-adult households.

Another issue directly related to sex roles is child rearing. Overall, there were few children who resided in the communes of the 1960s and 1970s. Zicklin (1983, p. 95) acknowledges that due to the lack of planning and spontaneous origin of communes there was little attention paid to collective child rearing. Most of the children present in communes during this time were infants and toddlers. The typical commune had two to five children, and they were normally taken care of by their mothers. As we have discussed earlier, egalitarianism did not generally extend into the domain of child care.

Communal families rarely provided children the alternative of a conventional family lifestyle (Constantine, 1977, p. 257). Larry Constantine (1977, p. 259) found that children reared in communes or what he called expanded families were "self-reliant but cooperative, competent more than competitive, friendly, robust, and self-confident." Charley M. Johnston and Robert W. Deisher (1973) reached similar conclusions as Constantine that commune children exhibited a high degree of maturity, self-confidence, and self-reliance. Berger (1981, p. 89) found commune children similar to other children, except that they had "saltier tongues." Fewer were shy and more seemed self-possessed in comparison to other middle-class children.

Similarities and differences between conventional and communal families were identified by Thomas S. Weisner and Joan C. Martin (1979, p. 236). Communal babies were breastfed more and were exposed to more caretakers. Both communal and conventional mothers were the primary caretakers and there were no differences in neonatal or infant physical growth and development or health. More research is needed on this topic and since these infants and toddlers are now adults themselves, it would be interesting to see if communal living has had any long term impact on their identities.

For the sake of cross-cultural comparison, we will now look briefly at the work of several sociologists and their findings regarding family life in communes in Great Britain during the 1960s and 1970s. Abrams and McCulloch (1976) and Rigby (1974) reached different interpretations of the communal movement in Great Britain. Rigby (1974) was much more positive and optimistic about the revolutionary potential and overall success of communes, while Abrams and McCulloch (1976) were much more pessimistic and skeptical about the impact of communes on British society. Abrams and McCulloch (1976, p. 151) saw communes as "alternative unrealities" primarily due to the issue of gender relationships. They concluded that communes had great difficulty unleashing themselves from the structures and constraints of traditional economic and moral society especially regarding gender relationships, thus producing unresolved conflict within what many were hoping would become utopian, egalitarian communities. Abrams and McCulloch (1976, p. 150) found that communes did not succeed in doing what is commonly known as family work any better than the traditional nuclear family, of which they were very critical.

Conclusion

While the majority of communes were in urban areas, it was the rural communes which attracted the attention of the media and the American public. Those who remained in the urban areas blended in with their surroundings, to a much greater extent, than their counterparts in rural

America. By the time urban communes were flourishing, rural communes were in decline and the American public had had its fill of alternative communities. The cultural revolution had not succeeded to the extent that many thought it would. America's young educated middle-class dropouts (following the edict of then Harvard psychologist Timothy Leary to "Turn on, tune in, and drop out") returned to modern society after searching for consensual community. Most failed to find it. Family life varied from commune to commune, sometimes being a major priority, while other times relegated to the sidelines.

Communal living was "hard on marriages" (Zablocki, 1980, p. 120). Of the 102 married couples who were tracked for a year during Zablocki's study, 47% were no longer living communally by the end of the year, and of the 54 couples who lived communally for a complete year, 57% were divorced or separated by the end of the year. The differences between secular and religious communes regarding the impact on marriage were significant. Only 27% of couples in secular communes were together after a year of study, while 76% of the couples in religious communes were together. Religious communes support and strengthen marriages (Zablocki, 1980, p. 345).

The use of commitment mechanisms varied from commune to commune and as Gardner (1978) reported, modern communes as a group used far fewer mechanisms to build commitment than nineteenth-century communal utopias. Surprisingly, while communalists were espousing the benefits of communal living, few actually were committed to communal sharing. While they were for the most part critical of the traditional nuclear family, they found it very difficult to shed their need for a family-like atmosphere where there was intimacy. Although they preached equality in sex roles, especially those who were creating secular communes, the majority of communes failed to enact structures that would facilitate that transition. Abrams and McCulloch's (1976, p. 150) conclusion, that British communes were not any better at family life than traditional nuclear families, can probably be said of American communes as well. The development of layered loyalties was a much more difficult task than the majority of communalists envisioned.

The pursuit of a gemeinschaft environment clashed with the gesellschaft socialization of these young radicals. For many, the variety of religious communes, with charismatic leaders, provided the structure and moral guidelines which they felt they needed to help them on their search for meaning in their lives, while secular communes came in all varieties as well.

One of the most important findings of Zablocki's (1980, p. 354) study was that charismatic renewal was a necessary ingredient for communal stability and survival. In their search for consensus, communal groups created networks of intense interpersonal interaction and in order to function properly these networks needed a healthy dose of charisma.

Communes of the 1960s and 1970s, in the end, were not a threat to the American family (Kephart, 1987, p. 288). Nor were they as radical as many had predicted. The high rates of membership turnover was an indicator that communes were frequently not as appealing as many were led to believe and/or wanted to believe. While the high failure rate is important, one must not lose sight that for some, communes provided a truly alternative lifestyle.

The next chapter will discuss urban and rural communes of the 1980s and 1990s. Many people think the communal movement is dead, but actually there are as many people living communally today than during the late 1960s and early 1970s. Jesus People USA, a religious commune in Chicago, and Twin Oaks, a secular rural commune in Virginia, will be highlighted. Although both of these communes originated before the 1980s, they are good examples of contemporary communal utopias. The chapter will also discuss the new communes which have developed during the last two decades of the twentieth century.

6

Urban and Rural Communes of
the 1980s and 1990s

In the 1980s, the United States continued to lead the world in the development of intentional communities, a case in point would be the phenomenal growth experienced by the Hutterites (Hutterian Brethren) (Oved, 1993, p. 482). Communes in the 1980s were not only surviving, but Oved (1993, p. 483) assessed the communal movement as stable and experiencing significant growth in comparison to the past. The communes of the 1960s were, for the most part, short-lived and transient, while those of the 1970s were a bit more stable and realistic in their goals (Oved, 1993, p. 481). The poor survival rate of the historic communes and those of the 1960s and 1970s has not negatively affected the rate at which new communities have been formed in the 1980s and 1990s.

New communal utopias will be created in response to the beginning of the third millennium (Pitzer, 1997, p. 500). The third millennium begins on January 1, 2001, and Pitzer and others, including Berry (1992, p. 241), expect significant communal development to take place among Adventist and apocalyptic groups as they prepare for, "the third millennium since the birth of Jesus and the prophetically significant seventh, and final millennium of Fundamentalist dispensationalism" (Pitzer, 1997, p. 500). Readers are reminded of the Branch Davidians, formed by charismatic leader David Koresh outside of Waco, Texas. Koresh and his followers were an apocalyptic religious movement preparing for the end of the world. The world did not end, but the Branch Davidians did. Their compound and its inhabitants perished in a fire after a 51-day standoff with the FBI. Koresh's followers apparently started the fire after FBI agents pumped tear gas into their buildings.

Apocalyptic millenarianism has recently become a more influential and powerful force as religious fundamentalists anticipate the final holocaust, including the "Rapture" and the battle of Armageddon. Apocalyptic millenarianism is attractive, to especially religious fundamentalists, because of the belief that secular forces are destroying the moral underpinnings of American society. The banning of prayer in public schools and the belief that secular humanism is being unleashed to dominate the curriculum in public schools, has mobilized fundamentalists into a vocal and influential voting block. These religionists believe the world has become sinful and corrupt because of the deterioration of traditional moral codes. Abortion, pornography, drugs, and sexual promiscuity are evidence, according to apocalyptic millenarianists, that the end of the world is near.

Paralleling the religious fanatics are the "secular prophets of doom." These groups claim that the end of the world is near as exhibited by the AIDS crisis, global warming, chemical weapons, etc. Additionally, Christian groups such as Amaeus Road Fellowship of Texas are withdrawing from what they view as a sinful and corrupt world. They are an agricultural commune of professionals who have left the secular and material world behind (Berry, 1992, p. 241).

The nuclear family is no longer viewed as a haven in a heartless world. Christopher Lasch (1979, p. xx) argues that the family has been deteriorating for more than 100 years and that the modern world has infiltrated it and shattered its privacy. The tension between work, family, and politics has reduced the family's effectiveness. Lasch (1979, p. xxiv) concludes that Americans can no longer retreat to their families for emotional security. He urges us to enact public policies that would restore family life. Communal living, for some, is a more viable attempt to create a life infused with values. Rather than run the risk of failure and frustration by trying to change the structure of nuclear family life and the conditions of public life, bonding together with others who are searching for the same thing is oftentimes more appealing.

There are currently between 3,000 and 4,000 communes (if communes are defined broadly to include cooperatives and cohousing), the vast majority of which have remained anonymous. Scholars can presently identify approximately 400 of these communes (These figures were provided by Donald Pitzer in the video, *Follow the Dirt Road: An Introduction to Intentional Communities in the 1990s* by Monique Gauthier, 1992 and D. Pitzer, personal communication, January 16, 1998). One group alone, the Hutterites, have over 400 colonies. There are hundreds of New Age communes, hundreds of Catholic monastic orders, land trusts, cooperatives, as well as cohousing developments. These numbers indicate that there probably are close to as many people living communally today as there were in any given year during the period from 1965 to 1975. As we discussed in Chapter 2, researchers such as Conover (1978) stated that there were 3,000 communes between 1971 and 1974 with 30,000 to 40,000 communalists. Richard Fairfield (1972) stated there were over 2,000 communes in 1969 to 1970, with an additional several thousand urban co-ops and collectives, while Zablocki (1980) found there were 1,000 rural communes in 1970. Granted, these were all estimates as are the current figures, but it appears that communal living is as popular today as it was during the 1960s and early 1970s even though it does not receive the attention or fanfare from the media that occurred in the 1960s and 1970s.

The media has spread the popular myth that communal living began with the hippies and died with the yuppies (young urban professionals), but Geoph Kozeny (1995, p. 18) states quite to the contrary, that there are thousands of groups today with hundreds of thousands of members living in communes (now frequently referred to as income-sharing communities) many of which resemble extended families which are not based on blood ties.

As discussed in Chapter 2, most of the active communes in the late 1990s are small, with fewer than 50 members. They have very diverse objectives and a wider range of orientations than those of the 1960s and 1970s, and even the 1980s. One of the most significant differences between communes of the 1990s and those of the 1960s and 1970s is that communalists tend not to reject the values of society, but select what they like from mainstream society and supplement their lives with those aspects of communal living which enhance and strengthen their sense of self (Berry, 1992, p. 243). Communal utopias of the 1990s and the first decade of the twenty-first century will focus more and more on issues related to health, the environment, stress reduction, personal morality, and building community. We will look at a cross section of these groups later in this chapter. These groups constitute a purposive sample of contemporary communal groups. My purpose in highlighting these groups is that they represent the various types of communes listed in the *Communities Directory.*

Urban Religious Communes of the 1980s

This section will focus on a study conducted by the author in Chicago during 1983 and is based primarily on the following sources (Smith, 1984; 1986; 1992; and 1994). Information on seven communes will be discussed summarizing their use of commitment mechanisms, their meaning systems, the impact of communal living on children, and members' impressions of whether or not the commune functioned as an extended family. While my focus in this section is on urban religious communes, it does not mean that urban secular and rural religious and secular did not exist; they did. I have chosen to concentrate on urban religious communes because of my extensive knowledge of them.

The following communes participated in the 1983 study of urban religious communes in Chicago: Austin Community Fellowship, Mennonite Volunteer Services: North of Howard Unit, Gospel Outreach, the Olive Branch, The Emissaries of Divine Light, Jesus People USA, and the Institute of Cultural Affairs. All of these communes, with the exception of the Emissaries of Divine Light, would be classified as Christian according to Zablocki's (1980, p. 205) commune ideologies discussed in Chapter 2. The Emissaries of Divine Light would be classified as more Eastern or consciousness oriented than Christian or direct action oriented. All of these communes, except for the Emissaries of Divine Light, were located within the City of Chicago. The Emissaries of Divine Light resided in a western suburb.

Austin Community Fellowship was founded in 1973 in the Austin neighborhood on the west side of the city. By the early 1980s, three communal households had disbanded and formed a church group. The financial resources and property of 14 adults and 16 children continued to be shared, but they resided in their own dwellings. In 1983 two families, four adults and six children, were sharing a home.

Mennonite Volunteer Services: North of Howard Unit was founded in 1982 and became a part of an ecumenical network of urban ministries called Good News North of Howard located in the Rogers Park neighborhood in northeast Chicago. This community of three women helped provide social services such as counseling and social support to people in this area of the city.

Gospel Outreach was organized in 1975 on the north side of the city in the Avondale neighborhood and is a network of Christian churches that minister to the needy and provide shelter and financial support for the homeless and distressed. They believe traditional denominational churches are too bureaucratized and do not practice the gospel. In 1983, nine adults and five children lived within two communal households.

The Emissaries of Divine Light were founded by Lloyd Meeker in 1932 and their international headquarters is in Loveland, Colorado. They are concerned with the spiritual regeneration of mankind. Six men and three women, including one married couple, share a household in a middle-class western suburb. This particular household was started in 1977. At one time, the community operated four communal households in the Chicago suburbs.

The Olive Branch was founded in 1876 and has been located at 1047 West Madison Avenue in the near west side neighborhood since 1927. It is one of the oldest missions in the country and its residents minister to people on Chicago's Skid Row. In 1983, 17 members, 14 adults and 3 children, lived communally at the mission. All of the adults were staff members who were required to live at the mission. The group believed that they needed the strength and security communal living provides to support them in their work with the poor and the rejected.

Jesus People USA was established in the Uptown neighborhood on the northeast side of the city in 1972. JPUSA is a nonprofit evangelical charismatic Christian fellowship. In 1983, 225 adults and 100 children lived communally. They minister to the poor and homeless and provide a daily meal and shelter for women and children in this blighted and neglected part of the city. Most of the adult members work in community-run enterprises.

The Institute of Cultural Affairs is an international ecumenical service organization. They are located at the corner of Sheridan and Lawrence in the Uptown neighborhood not far from Jesus People USA. There are over 100 offices throughout the world and the Chicago office is one of five coordinating centers. In 1983, 120 adults and 90 children lived

TABLE 6.1 Summary of Commitment Scores

	ACF	MVS	GO	OB	EDL	JPUSA	ICA
SACRIFICE	1	1	3	1	1	3	0
INVESTMENT	2	0	0	0	1	1	0
RENUNCIATION	0	0	0	0	0	0	0
COMMUNION	8	9	8	11	12	12	7
MORTIFICATION	4	2	6	4	5	7	6
TRANSCENDENCE	4	4	6	6	5	6	7
TOTAL	19	16	23	22	24	29	20

	Mean (Smith)	Mean (Kanter)	Mean (Gardner)
SACRIFICE	1.4	2.17	8.69
INVESTMENT	.6	3.13	3.69
RENUNCIATION	0	4.26	12.77
COMMUNION	9.6	10.80	22.31
MORTIFICATION	4.8	5.43	2.62
TRANSCENDENCE	5.4	10.93	6.33

NOTE: ACF = Austin Community Fellowship; MVS = Mennonite Volunteer Services; GO = Gospel Outreach; OB = Olive Branch; EDL = Emissaries of Divine Light; JPUSA = Jesus People USA; ICA = Institute of Cultural Affairs. For a detailed explanation of the various measures of commitment see Smith (1984; 1986).

communally. The Institute of Cultural Affairs was originally part of the Ecumenical Institute which was formed by the World Council of Churches, but became a separate entity in 1973.

Table 6.1 displays the commitment scores of the seven communes, as well as a summary of the scores found by Kanter (1972) and Gardner (1978) in their respective studies of nineteenth-century groups and rural communes of the 1960s and 1970s.

Sacrifice is the third least used mechanism, with a mean score of (1.4). Jesus People USA and the Mennonite Volunteer Services groups indicated their living conditions are austere. Most of the groups do not abstain from certain foods. Married couples are not required to abstain from sex with their spouses, although four of the communes require their single members to abstain from sexual relations.

The Institute of Cultural Affairs does not use any form of sacrifice, while Gospel Outreach and Jesus People USA use three forms of sacrifice. Jesus People USA requires members to abstain from smoking, alcohol, and recreational drugs. Sexual abstinence is expected of single members and extramarital sex is forbidden. Gospel Outreach members are asked to abstain from any habit and single members are required to refrain from sex.

Investment is the second least used commitment mechanism, with a mean score of (0.6). Austin Community Fellowship and the Emissaries of Divine Light restrict nonresident participation, while financial investment is encouraged by Jesus People USA and Austin Community Fellowship. None of the groups return all of the property or financial investment of members who leave the commune.

Renunciation is not used by any of the groups. Couples and families are not renounced and the communal households are not isolated from society. This is a significant difference from communes of previous decades.

The most utilized commitment mechanisms are communion, transcendence, and mortification with the following mean scores of (9.6), (5.4), and (4.8). Homogeneity, communal sharing, communal labor, and regularized group contact are measures most frequently used among the groups to build communion. Homogeneity was the most used single communion measure. A middle-class socioeconomic background and a white European ethnic background are traits that reinforce homogeneity which are shared especially by members of the Olive Branch and the Emissaries of Divine Light. Jesus People USA, the Emissaries of Divine Light, the Mennonite Volunteer Services, and the Austin Community Fellowship use a common purse (pooling of money and income of the group to pay the bills, etc.). Jesus People USA is financed through the combined labor of its members in a variety of communal business enterprises (painting, roofing, electrical, moving, carpentry, etc.). The kitchen at JPUSA is also a communal undertaking. Meals, especially the evening meal, are shared by members as is common in all of these groups.

Transcendence is exhibited most readily by six of these groups regarding the importance of ideological conversion to group beliefs and practices. Fixed daily routines and a hierarchy of authority are used by the majority of these communal utopias.

Mortification is practiced most frequently through confession and mutual criticism. Austin Community Fellowship, Gospel Outreach, Jesus People USA, and the Institute of Cultural Affairs incorporate these aspects of mortification into their daily life. Sanctions and spiritual differentiation are the two most popular forms of mortification commitment. For example, Jesus People USA and the Institute of Cultural Affairs expelled members from their communes.

There is no difference in the use of continuance (sacrifice and investment) mechanisms between the large and small groups. While no groups used renunciation mechanisms, there are no differences in the use of communion mechanisms between the large and small groups. The larger communes used more mortification mechanisms, but the difference between them and the smaller communes is minimal. There are no major differences between the large and small groups in their use of transcendence mechanisms.

The mean score for the number of commitment mechanisms used by these communes is 22. Jesus People USA used 29, while Mennonite Volunteer Services used 16. The number of mechanisms used is not influenced by the longevity of the group. The two smallest groups had the lowest commitment scores. These low scores can be accounted for in part by the temporary arrangement (1 year) of these groups. Jesus People USA, the largest group, attained the highest score, while the Institute of Cultural Affairs, the second largest group, used nine fewer mechanisms. This can be explained by the more transient nature of the Institute of Cultural Affairs. A large number of its members are there on a temporary basis and their focus is not on long-term commitment to that specific location, while at JPUSA members have much more permanency.

Communion, transcendence, and mortification are used by urban religious communes at moderate levels or better, while sacrifice and investment are not widely used and renunciation is nonexistent. Kanter (1972) found that nineteenth-century communes used transcendence and communion mechanisms the most, followed by sacrifice, renunciation, investment, and mortification. Gardner (1978) found that modern rural communes used investment, renunciation, and mortification mechanisms, while sacrifice, communion, and transcendence were weakly or negatively related to communal survival in the 1960s and 1970s.

The majority of urban religious communalists in Chicago expected to live in their respective communities for their entire life or at least for a long extended period. Prayer was the most utilized form of religious activity by these communards, followed by Sunday worship, and reading the Bible. Regarding their religious meaning system, they believed that Divine Grace, friends, parents, and reading were the most important influences by which they acquired their spiritual and religious beliefs. Since living communally, the majority of members believed the single most important change in their lifestyle, personality, or personal identity was that they felt more secure about themselves.

One reason why communal groups might have a richer meaning system is due to their use of commitment mechanisms. Commitment mechanisms may manifestly or latently enhance their meaning systems. Because primary groups are usually all-purpose groups and communes are primary groups, one would expect commitment mechanisms to play a significant role in securing the strong emotional and companionship ties which are essential for communal living. These commitment mechanisms act as plausibility structures which reinforce meaning systems. The meaning system is held in common and it is fortified because the group supports it and the individual's spiritual quest within the larger world view. A theme permeating their responses is that God has given them an identity and direction and their communities reinforce and enhance their consistent walk with the Lord. The "miracle of Christian community" is possible because of the Bible and Christ's life. Because of these, people from different backgrounds and life experiences can live together.

Four of the communes (Austin Community Fellowship, the Olive Branch, Jesus People USA, and the Institute of Cultural Affairs) included children. The parents (32 adults—22 females and 10 males) had a total of 60 children (36 males and 24 females) living with them in the commune. The children ranged in age from 2 months to 19 years of age. A closer look revealed 6 children were under 1-year-old, 43 were 1 through 10-years-old, and 9 were 11 through 19-years-old. Two children identified by one respondent were actually adults who happened to be living within the same communal household as their parent.

TABLE 6.2 Effects of Communal Living on Children[a]

Effects	Number of Responses
1. outgoing, not shy	(3)
2. highly stimulated	(1)
3. trusting	(3)
4. good communication skills with children and adults	(4)
5. secure, belonging, sense of community	(7)
6. global consciousness	(5)
7. coping skills, stability	(4)
8. accepting of other races, nonprejudiced	(5)
9. sense of service to others	(2)
10. greater awareness of social issues	(1)
11. sharing belongings and time	(5)
12. independent	(1)
13. strong peer leadership in older children	(3)
14. imaginative, intelligent, articulate, innovative	(2)
15. Christian atmosphere	(1)
16. sheltered	(1)
17. consistency in love, discipline, morals, they know what is expected	(5)
18. not competitive	(1)
19. happy	(1)
20. learn faster	(1)
21. open	(1)
22. better behavior	(2)
23. structured playtime	(1)
24. socially advance	(2)
25. more help available for social problems	(2)
26. gets lots of attention	(1)
27. not afraid of strangers	(1)
28. lack of emotional space	(1)
29. overly competitive	(1)

SOURCE: From *SYZYGY: Journal of Alternative Religion and Culture* (p. 56), by W. L. Smith, 1994. © 1994 by the Center for Academic Publication. Reprinted with permission.
a. Some respondents mentioned more than one effect.

Respondents were asked the following question: Are there any particular ways in which living here has had an effect on your children? In addition, the following contingency question was asked: If yes, specify how the community has had an effect on your children. Table 6.2 identifies the effects of communal living on the children of these four communes.

Seven parents mentioned their children felt more secure in the commune, that the children had a strong sense they belonged there, and that the children had a sense of community, meaning they realized they were connected to something much larger than their nuclear family. Five parents identified that living in community enhanced their children's sense of global consciousness, aided them in accepting people of other races and ethnicities, contributed to a nonprejudiced view of life, encouraged them to share belongings and time, and provided the basis for some consistency in love, discipline, and morals. Last but not least, children knew what was expected of them. Four parents noted communal living fostered good communication skills with other children and adults, assisted children in learning coping skills, as well as provided a stable environment for them. Three parents identified their children as being more outgoing, trusting, and not shy; while older children developed strong leadership capabilities. Two parents mentioned communal living had created a sense of service to others, they noticed their children were socially advanced, and benefited from the help available in the commune for social problems. There was little variation between the four communes regarding the effects of communal living on children. Parents' responses where not significantly different based on their length of membership and gender.

Three of the communities (Austin Community Fellowship, Jesus People USA, and the Institute of Cultural Affairs) indicated the other adults besides the child's parent are responsible for child care within the community. Zablocki (1980, p. 349) found that among the urban communes he studied in the 1960s and 1970s, 33% of parents were responsible for their own children, 42% shared child care responsibilities with other members, 14% used communal day care, and 11% of the children related to all adults as if they were parents.

There are multiple similarities between Austin Community Fellowship, Jesus People USA, the Olive Branch, and the Institute of Cultural Affairs, and the communes of the 1960s and 1970s regarding children. The children seemed sensitive to the needs of others, they felt secure, they had good communication skills, and they were accepting of others. Zablocki (1980) found parents were positive about the impact of communal living on their children as did the Chicago communalists. A total of 84% of the Chicago communalists believed communal living enhanced their relationship with their children. Zicklin's (1983) findings in reference to religious communes and parent-child relations coincide with those of the urban religious communes in Chicago. Parents are the primary caretakers, but they rely on others within the commune as well as communal day care to supervise their children in their absence.

Nuclear families were incorporated into the everyday life of six of the groups. The only one not incorporating nuclear families was the Mennonite Volunteer Services: North of Howard Unit. This occurred for the sole reason that there were none, the group consisted of three single women. All of the six communes with nuclear families provided them with separate sleeping quarters, although both Austin Community Fellowship and the Emissaries of Divine Light stated that young children from different families have shared rooms.

The communities were asked how they incorporated nuclear families into communal life. Although meals are communal at Jesus People USA, nuclear families sit together and they have special times set aside just for them. Parents are encouraged to interact with their children often. At the Olive Branch, nuclear families participate in meals, worship services, and celebrations, while at Gospel Outreach the community encourages nuclear families and does not hinder their family time. The Emissaries of Divine Light emphasized that they are one family, but space is made for nuclear families to live somewhat as an "individual family" if that is what they desire. While this is encouraged, the community does not want nuclear families to segregate themselves away from others.

The marital status of the 86 adults who responded to the second of two questionnaires used to gather data for the initial study (Smith, 1984) is as follows: 29 were single and never married, 44 were married, 2 were separated, 8 were divorced, and 3 were widowed.

The following discussion is based on the responses these 86 communalists gave to the two questions in Table 6.3.

Table 6.4, "The Influence of Community on Intimate Relationships" and Table 6.5, "Communal Household Functions as an Extended Family" summarize the responses to these two questions. The responses were 67 communalists stated that communal living enhanced their relationships with fellow community friends, 42 with their parents, 41 with their

TABLE 6.3 Survey Questions

1. Has community life enhanced and fostered the development and bonding of close intimate relationships? (Mark appropriate responses)

_____ Between you and your spouse

_____ Between you and your children

_____ Between you and community friends

_____ Between you and your parents

_____ Between you and non-community friends

_____ Between you and your natural brothers and sisters

_____ Other (specify) _____

2. Do you feel this communal household functions as an extended family? (Select one)

_____ Always

_____ Usually

_____ Sometimes

_____ Seldom

_____ Never

spouses, 36 with their children (28 of the 32 parents responded that community life enhanced their relationship with their children, the 8 additional respondents have children who do not reside with them), 35 with their brothers and sisters, 30 with noncommunity friends, and 10 with others.

The following are unsolicited written comments provided by three members of Jesus People USA regarding the influence of community life on their relationships:

> I think being involved in a community has enhanced all my relationships as it has helped me to grow as a person. Especially being a Christian, which is really, for me, the essential factor.

> I do believe through my growth and maturity over the years my relationship with my mother has changed and we understand each other as two mature adults. My sisters were all older than me. I left home at 15 so our relationship was never too close to begin with although we are friendly, write, and visit when possible.

TABLE 6.4 The Influence of Community on Intimate Relationships

	S	C	CF	P	NCF	B&S	O	Total
ACF	4	4	3	2	0	1	0	14
MVS	0	0	0	0	1	0	2	3
GO	2	1	5	3	4	2	0	17
EDL	0	0	5	2	2	2	2	13
OB	3	3	8	0	4	2	2	22
JPUSA	22	17	33	26	11	19	3	131
ICA	10	11	13	9	8	9	1	61
TOTAL	41	36	67	42	30	35	10	261

NOTE: ACF = Austin Community Fellowship; MVS = Mennonite Volunteer Services; GO = Gospel Outreach; EDL = Emissaries of Divine Light; OB = Olive Branch; JPUSA = Jesus People USA; ICA = Institute of Cultural Affairs
NOTE: S = Spouse; C = Children; CF = Community Friends; P = Parents; NCF = Non-Community Friends; B&S = Brothers and Sisters; O = Other

TABLE 6.5 Communal Household Functions as an Extended Family

	A	U	ST	S	N
ACF	0	2	3	0	0
MVS	0	1	1	0	1
GO	2	2	1	0	0
EDL	2	2	0	0	1
OB	2	6	1	1	0
JPUSA	26	8	1	0	0
ICA	8	8	4	2	1
TOTAL	40	29	11	3	3

NOTE: ACF = Austin Community Fellowship; MVS = Mennonite Volunteer Services; GO = Gospel Outreach; EDL = Emissaries of Divine Light; OB = Olive Branch; JPUSA = Jesus People USA; ICA = Institute of Cultural Affairs
NOTE: A = Always; U = Usually; ST = Sometimes; S = Seldom; N = Never

They (brothers and sisters) respect me a lot more because I take care of my family in a way that suits them. I used to be pretty harsh with my children even though they were quite young. They disrespect me because they think I think I'm better than them. I disagree with a lot of their moral stands such as adultery, drinking, etc. and they think I'm being too harsh. The only reason I verbalize my feelings toward them is that I too rise to do such things and have had to face the consequences in a way most unpleasing. They don't see it as I'm trying to spare them a lot of hurt, but as self-righteousness. I'm very sad about this as I don't usually start these conversations but they ask my opinion about such actions.

Regarding whether they feel the communal household functions as an extended family, 40 said always, 29 usually, 11 sometimes, 3 seldom, and 3 never. Of the 32 parents who have children present with them, 14 said always, 11 usually, 6 sometimes, 0 seldom, and 1 never. These figures mirror the overall responses of communal members.

The following unsolicited comments were provided regarding the extended family:

The body of Christ is a family, because we have become sons and daughters of God. The family of God is much closer, warmer, and committed than the "extended" family of blood relationships which exists in the world. I can go anywhere in the world and Christians will welcome me in their household as a sister, even though they have never met me or even heard of me before. This has nothing to do with being part of an organization or a church. Christians who have traveled will tell you the same thing. Our little communal house was just a small part of God's family all over the world. We are "blood relations" by the blood of Jesus Christ. This concept of family is a difficult thing for an unsaved person (someone who has not yet received Jesus as their personal Lord and savior) to grasp. But the person can sit down at a meal with Christians and pick up a sense of family right away, a sense of love and freedom, warmth and honesty, closeness, that he hasn't sensed in non-Christian families. (Gospel Outreach)

It is what it is not an extension of anything to me. Family is a good word for it. (Emissaries of Divine Light)

In a sense there are many extended families within the community, but our commitment to one another is that of family as opposed to institutional or organizational. (Jesus People USA)

Community life does impact the intimate relationships of these group members in a myriad of ways, not always to the liking of the individual. While the individual from Jesus People USA wrote her brothers and sisters respected her for the positive change in her parenting skills, they dismissed her as "preachy" and "self-righteous" when she chastised them for their immoral behavior. While the members believe the communal household functions as an extended family, they really mean the relational or social psychological ties are there, more so than structural ties. This is clearly evident by the comment of the person from Gospel Outreach.

Communes of the 1990s

This section is based on some recent work I have done on the contemporary communal movement (Smith, 1996a).

The most comprehensive source for information on communal living in the 1990s is the 1995 edition of the *Communities Directory: A Guide to Cooperative Living*. This guide identifies 550 North American communities (29 in Canada, 4 in Mexico, and 516 in the United States) and 69 international communities (13 in Australia and 13 in the United Kingdom, while the other 20 countries average 2 communities each). An additional 150 communities were identified, but they asked not to be included in the directory.

Urban and rural communes are located throughout the United States, but the following states have the largest concentrations: California (94), New York (34), Washington (27), Massachusetts and Virginia (23 each), Colorado and Wisconsin (22 each), Pennsylvania (20), and Missouri and Arizona (19 each). About one third of the communities identify themselves as religious or spiritual and representatives of the following groups can be found among them: Sufi, Christian, Eastern, Pagan, Roman Catholic, Buddhist, Humanist, New Age, New Social Order in Messiah, Protestant, Hutterian Brethren, Ecumenical, Eclectic, Emissaries of Divine Light, Native American Indian, Hare Krishna, Jewish, Unitarian Universalist, Sikh/Yogic, Yoga, and others.

The primary purposes or foci of the communes varies as can be seen by the following labels used by the groups to identify themselves: equality, ecology, good life; extended family, group process; shared spiritual life; collective co-ownership; personal growth, social justice; lesbian feminist; self-actualization, service; cohousing; based on vow of nonviolence; diversity, cooperation, stewardship; peace and human rights; living together creatively; inexpensive rural co-op living; cooperative urban household; meditation practice and study; permanent family-like home; family, ecology, wholeness; sustainable living; radical Christian community; contemplative practice; yoga and Vedanta; shared community living; rural community land trust; and well-being, equality, self-sufficiency.

Twin Oaks and Jesus People USA have been in existence for over 25 years and they are good examples of a secular/rural contemporary commune and an urban/religious contemporary commune. Twin Oaks would fit under Zablocki's (1980, p. 205) rubric of primary group community overlapping the ideologies of cooperative and alternative family, while Jesus People USA fits solidly among Christian communes. If judged by longevity alone, these two communes are among the most successful currently existing in the United States.

Twin Oaks was established in 1967 and it is one of the oldest secular intentional communities in the United States. Although originally inspired by the book *Walden Two* by B. F. Skinner, the community has since abandoned its connection with the major ideas (especially behaviorism) espoused by Skinner. It is located in rural Louisa, Virginia and consists of 85 adults, 55% of whom are women. In addition there are 14 children under the age of 19. In the early years, children lived in a children's house until they were of school age and the community was responsible for child rearing. This has changed and parents are now responsible for their own children. Twin Oaks has always been ambivalent about the nuclear family, neither condemning or supporting it. In the early 1970s, some members attempted to create surrogate families in a branch experiment called Merion. It failed after several years. Legal marriage, lifelong monogamy, and celibacy are not common at Twin Oaks. The commune owns the land which consists of 460 acres. Nearly all of their meals are eaten communally and they grow nearly 50% of their food. Children are either home-schooled or attend private or public schools. Their primary purpose and focus is equality, ecology, and nonviolence. Twin Oaks is economically self-sufficient. Most members do a variety of work including making hammocks and furniture, indexing books, making tofu, milking cows, farming, cooking, and child care (see Kinkade, 1973 and 1994; Komar, 1983).

Jesus People USA (discussed earlier) is an urban commune located in Chicago whose focus is evangelical Christian ministry. In 1989, JPUSA joined the Evangelical Covenant Church which is a denomination related to the Evangelical Free Church. They were formed in 1972 and there are presently 350 adults, half of whom are women, and 150 children under the age of 19. The commune owns several large buildings, income is shared, and a group of elders directs the community. Nearly all of their meals are taken communally and children are community-schooled. Community-owned businesses provide 90% of the community's income and they operate a 56-bed shelter for homeless women and children, as well as provide 200 hot meals daily to street people. Individual nuclear families have their own small apartments in a large building owned by the community. They are very supportive of nuclear families, but expect them to work together along with singles to foster community. JPUSA are the producers of *Cornerstone Magazine* and sponsor several bands (heavy metal, rap, punk rock, and Irish/Celtic folk) as well as the Cornerstone Festival which is held each summer in a suburban Chicago community.

The groups in Table 6.6 represent a collection of co-ops, collectives, communes, intentional communities, utopian groups, and religious as well as secular communities. They mirror the other communities discussed in the *Communities Directory*. Within this collection, one will find direct action- and consciousness-oriented groups as we discussed in Chapter 2. For the vast majority of these 10 groups, decisions regarding their communal life are made by consensus and most share a least two or three communal meals a week. Several groups share all of their meals together. Children attend public, private, and community-operated schools, while some are home-schooled.

Of the 550 North American communes, 24 specifically or approximately 4% state that their primary purpose and/or focus is family related (see Table 6.7). As of 1995, nine of these groups are in the process of forming and two are reforming. Almost half of these family related communes are just beginning to operate as communes. Might this be a prognostication of things to come? Are we beginning to see a shift in focus

TABLE 6.6 A Selection of Communes From the 1990s

Name/Location/Started/Type/Population/Purpose

---

1. Hei Wa House/MI/1985/urban cooperative household/8 adults
2. Lama Foundation/NM/1968/rural ecumenical and eclectic spiritual commune/ 8 adults and one child/awakening of one's consciousness
3. N Street Cohousing/CA/1986/urban intentional community/32 adults and 16 children
4. One World Family Commune/CA/1967/rural and urban commune/13 adults and 2 children/world transformation and utopia
5. Whole Health Foundation/CA/1973/urban commune/10 adults/ holistic group vegetarian home
6. Birdsfoot Farm/NY/1972/rural commune/11 adults/vegetarians
7. Cardiff Place/Ontario,, CANADA/1994/urban cohousing community/16 adults and 6 children
8. Fairview House (Folks)/CA/1992/urban commune/13 adults and 3 children/ affordable progressive community
9. Women's Co-op/WI/1991/urban co-op/8 adults/women's cooperative
10. Green Pastures Estate/NH/1963/rural commune/67 adults and 5 children/ spiritual group

---

SOURCE: This table was derived from information provided in the *Communities Directory: A Guide to Cooperative Living* compiled by the Fellowship for Intentional Community (1995).

from that of consensual community, as reported by Zablocki (1980), to that of extended families, as indicated by Kanter and Halter (1973b)? Of the 24 groups, 8 emphasized they were extended families. Obviously, more research will need to be conducted before we can make a definitive statement, but it appears at this point in time there is some movement toward a larger emphasis on structural and interactional family ties. Another important point to consider is that many more of the 550 intentional communities, besides the 24 listed in Table 6.7, might also be interested in developing family ties but as secondary or latent goals as discussed by Zablocki (1980, p. 202). After reading through the brief descriptions of the intentional communities provided in the second part of the *Communities Directory,* I believe this to be true.

For those interested in more information on intentional communities, the Fellowship for Intentional Communities has a Web page: http://www.ic.org or you reach them by e-mail at fic@ic.org.

TABLE 6.7 Contemporary Communes With a Family Focus

Name and Location	Focus
1. Agape Lay Apostololate Cmty (NM)	prayer service family
2. Alpha Farm (OR)	extended family, group processes
3. Black Oak Ranch (CA)	humor, friendship, extended family
4. Bright Morning Star (WA) (RF)	musical loving close family
5. Caerduir (MO) (F)	family independence earth-care
6. Covenental Cmty (IL)	Christian urban extended family
7. Crosses Creek (AR)	to be a family
8. Earth Re-leaf (HI) (RF)	consensus land trust and family
9. Folkhaven (AK) (F)	family tribe and folk
10. The Good Red Road (CA) (F)	growth, family, sharing, security
11. Harmon House (CA)	ecological, family, stability, friendly, food
12. Heartwinds (CA) (F)	good neighbors friends family
13. Hillegass House (CA)	communal family-like living
14. International Puppydogs (OR) (F)	extended intimate family
15. L'Arche Mobile (AL)	permanent family-like home
16. Prairie Ridge Cmty (WI) (F)	family, ecology, wholeness
17. Recreation Center (HI)	family entertainment and fun
18. Rowanwood (Canada)	extended family, caring, stewardship
19. Six Directions (UT) (F)	Optimal family health (eclectic)
20. Society of Family Solidarity (CA) (F)	enhancement of fraternal families
21. Songaia Cmty (WA)	earth centered extended family
22. Syntony (HI) (F)	family clusters, networking, polyfidelity
23. The Vale (OH)	family and environment centered
24. Whitehall Co-op (TX)	support, family bonding

SOURCE: This table was derived from the North American Cross-Reference Chart in the *Communities Directory: A Guide to Cooperative Living* by the Fellowship for Intentional Community (1995).
NOTE: (F) = forming; (RF) = reforming

Conclusion

Based on the number of intentional communities operating today and the number of new groups created in the last decade, communal living is alive and well in the late 1990s. Scholars anticipate that there is the potential for even more growth as the third millennium approaches. The largest communal group in the United States, the Hutterites, continues to grow and create new colonies at an unprecedented rate. There are probably as many people living in intentional communities today, as were in the late 1960s and early 1970s. Jesus People USA is a good example of an intentional community which has developed layered loyalties which link nuclear families to the group. They nurture the nuclear family, while at the same time utilizing commitment mechanisms which link individuals and families to the community.

While urban religious communes of the 1980s did not use as many commitment mechanisms as nineteenth century communes and rural communes of the 1960s and 1970s, they did not renounce the nuclear family as did many of the historic communes and rural communes of the 1960s and 1970s. Family life is important to groups like Jesus People USA and the Hutterites.

Parents in the urban religious communes I studied are positive about the impact communal living has on their children. They indicated that community life had a direct positive effect on a variety of their intimate relationships. These communalists overwhelmingly agreed that their communes functioned as extended families.

We find as much diversity in structure and form among the communities of the 1990s as in previous decades. One third of the North American communes listed in the *Communities Directory* are religious or spiritual in orientation, while 4% of them indicated that family life is their primary purpose or focus. Almost half of the 24 communities that specified family as a primary focus or purpose are in the process of forming. Nontraditional family settings are as popular today as they have ever been. The future of communal living and families in intentional communities looks bright.

The next and final segment of this book, Chapter 7, "What Have We Learned About Families and Communes?" will provide a summary of the most salient material presented in this book and a brief discussion regarding the future of communes.

7

What Have We Learned About Families and Communities?

Our examination and analysis of families and communes is drawing to a close, but before we end our conversation about them we need to take stock of the key points discussed in the previous chapters. This summarization should assist us in assessing our understanding of family life within intentional communities.

We have learned that communes vary greatly from one another, as indicated by Zablocki's (1980, p. 205) typology and by applications of Kanter's (1972) theory of commitment. There is no typical communal setting and family life within communes is diverse. Some communes are better suited for marriage and family life than others. Zablocki (1980) found high rates of marital dissolution in secular communes, while membership in religious communes apparently strengthened marriage and family life. Communalists of the 1960s and 1970s were raised in loving and intimate two-parent households. Within these families the future communalists learned the capacity to trust, an essential component for successful communal living. In light of these findings, it makes perfect sense that the communalists were more concerned with building consensual community than reconstructing new families. For most, communal living was a temporary episode in their lives. An interlude before settling down in a more traditional arrangement. Not surprisingly, Ferrar (1982) reported that parents of young children were more likely to stay in communes where family life was a central, rather than an incidental concern.

The communal utopias most likely to survive are religious, use commitment mechanisms, control access and admission to the commune, and limit the degree of sexual freedom of members (Kanter, 1972; Zablocki, 1980). In addition, Mowery (1978) found that communes which are well financed, rather than those existing at the subsistence level, survive. Highly structured communes last longer than anarchistic communes. Successful communes develop social processes within their social structures which build, what Etzioni (1996) refers to as, "layered loyalties."

Family Versus Community

Most communes, whether historic or contemporary, have not abolished the family. Only a minority of communal utopias have adopted celibacy, monasticism, or some type of complex marriage such as pantagamy as exhibited by the Oneida community. Owenite and Fourierist communes criticized families, but they did not abolish them. Icaria welcomed families and viewed them as integral components for the long-term survival of the community.

Amana, while at first hesitant because of its theology, incorporated nuclear families as a necessity for survival. The Shakers abolished the family, but the community assumed the usual functions provided by nuclear families.

Most of the groups which abandoned family life and adopted celibacy did so for religious reasons. After the religious fervor of the early 1800s ebbed, most religious communes exhibited what would be called traditional family life. The Hutterites, who arrived in the United States toward the end of the 1800s, are an excellent example of a religious group that has maintained and depends on the nuclear family. While some feminists might not approve of their patriarchal structure and limited roles for women, the Hutterites, nevertheless, exemplify a communal group that has reconciled the dilemma between family and community (Oved, 1993).

Communal utopias have introduced society to new family forms such as the "post-biological family," but they have not replaced the nuclear family, nor are they likely to. The nuclear family, as we know it in the United States, has undergone an immense amount of change due mostly to the impact of divorce, remarriage, out-of-wedlock births, and the economy. These changes have altered the physical structure of the American family, as well as its social psychological configuration. Many participants in contemporary intentional communities are attracted to them not only because of the group's structure, but because they learn how to enrich their familial relationships through their communal membership. Communal membership provides individuals and families the opportunity to share a common life with others who have similar values and goals. Communal living is also attractive to those who are interested in sharing resources, especially single parents.

Intimate relationships are no longer only relegated to the nuclear family. By intimate, I do not mean solely sexual relationships, but intimate in a very broad sense. Obviously, sexual relationships outside of one's marriage are destructive. Zablocki's (1980) findings are very clear on that issue, but spouses are not the only people we can rely on to have close nonsexual relationships. The old conception of love relegated intimacy to the marriage, while the modern conception of love acknowledges that family members need to develop healthy intimate relationships with those outside of their immediate families too. These relationships in turn enhance those within the family (Reiss, 1980, p. 130). While surely not the only place or source for relationships, intentional communities provide an outlet for these types of important relationships that are necessary for healthy family and community life. These intimate relationships are the "layered loyalties" which weave individuals, families, and communities together.

Communities which have survived the test of time are those that have found some balance between maintaining social order and personal autonomy. All of the communes we have investigated have dealt with this issue, some were more successful than others. The development of social processes that create "layered loyalties" between the individual and community or the family and community are necessary for the long-term success of any intentional community (Etzioni, 1996).

Kanter's (1972) theory of commitment provided us with a useful measuring stick to assess the impact social processes had on maintaining social order, while integrating individuals and families into community life. We found that the use of commitment mechanisms (sacrifice, investment, renunciation, communion, mortification, and transcendence) varied from commune to commune and also from epoch to epoch. The adoption and use of these mechanisms influenced the structure of social life within these communities.

While the use of commitment mechanisms welded individuals, families, and communities together, it was the ideology of the group which influenced how family, gender roles, work, parental roles, sexual relationships, leadership, and child rearing would be conceptualized. Religious communes tended to be much more traditional regarding family issues than secular communes, although John Humphrey Noyes and the Oneida Community are exceptions to the rule. Other exceptions to the rule include Shaker women who commanded certain authority that normally would have been only given to men in traditional societies. Contemporary Hutterite women occupy some leadership positions, but these are usually in more traditional areas of family life such as cooking, cleaning, and child care. While rural communes often have more liberal policies on sex, they are more likely to be traditional regarding gender, work, and parental roles. Rural communalists of the 1960s and 1970s were not as fully liberated as they thought or as myth reveals. Religious communes are frequently guided by charismatic leaders, while nonanarchistic secular communes are consensus driven.

Are nuclear families a threat to communal life? Kanter (1972, p. 90) found that successful nineteenth century communes were more likely to dissolve the nuclear family than nonsuccessful communes. While this is true, one can argue that these successful communes also used more commitment mechanisms to bind the individual to the community than did modern communes. Might the real issue here be not whether families are present or not, but how well communities weave individuals into the fabric of community life? I think so. While families can be sources of conflict for communities and compete with them for the loyalty of individuals, they can also provide useful services that communities are not necessarily equipped to provide, such as affective satisfaction. Successful communes are those that incorporate families rather than exclude them. Several excellent examples are Amana, the Hutterites, and Jesus People USA. While Amana is no longer an intentional community, its church life provides the necessary continuity and connection to its past.

Even though Amana ceased to exist as a communal group in the 1930s, Pitzer (1997a) argues that they are a good example to explain the new emerging theory of developmental communalism. Developmental communalism stresses the importance of studying communal utopias as social movements and the need to examine them over time, from their beginning, to the end of their communal stage, and beyond. Pitzer (1997a, p. 13) acknowledges that this new theory moves beyond the confining limits imposed by those who judge communes as successful solely by their longevity, to looking at success as determined by how well they achieved their goals, took care of their members, and influenced society.

Developmental communalism appears to be closely linked to two sociological approaches to the study of social movements, the collective behavior approach and the resource mobilization approach. Stark (1998, p. 582) argues that when these two approaches are combined together, they provide a viable means of explaining how social movements occur and succeed. The collective behavior approach emphasizes that social movements are created by reactions to grievances, while the resource mobilization approach emphasizes the role of human and material resources, as well as planning as the source of social movements.

Scholars who use developmental communalism explain,

> Why certain movements chose the discipline of communal living to survive or to implement a utopian plan and why certain of them later moved beyond the close fellowship and collective strength of a communal period into other ways of organizing that proved better for their movement's development. (Pitzer, 1997a, p. 12)

The theory of developmental communalism appears to fit well as an explanatory framework for Amana and the Onedia Community. Scholars using this framework would conclude that these communal utopias were successful. As the reader will remember, both of these communal utopias formed joint-stock companies after the dissolution of communal life. While Amana maintained nuclear families throughout its existence, Oneida practiced complex marriage until the end. One can assume that the dissolution of communal living was more dramatic for the Oneida Community primarily because they also ended the practice of pantagamy. As we discussed earlier in Chapter 3, both Amana and Oneida struggled with the influence of nuclear families on the community. In both cases, it appears that a few powerful families did exert a considerable amount of influence within these communities, but neither communal utopia dissolved only because of these families.

As we have discussed before, marriage and family life does impact and is impacted by communal living. Zablocki's (1980) findings have been reported previously in this chapter regarding the difference between religious and secular communes. The research I conducted in 1983 revealed that close to one half of the respondents indicated that community life enhanced their relationship with their spouse.

While I did not ask the respondents to discuss the quality of their marriages, several individuals indicated their marriages were in trouble and they were hoping communal living would help mend their relationships. It is conceivable to believe that some of these couples had sought traditional remedies, such as marriage counseling. I know that several of the communes had trained marriage counselors among their members.

Communal ideology influences not only gender and work roles, but also whether marriage and family life are compatible with communal living and vice versa. At the same time, those groups which abolished the formal nuclear family, such as the Shakers, created defacto substitutes. The various Shaker families, within each of the 23 Shaker villages, became the equivalent of the abandoned nuclear family. As we discussed in Chapter 3, sisters often performed tasks for the brothers and vice versa mirroring what spouses would do for each other. Besides sharing tasks, brothers and sisters probably also developed what Hillery (1992, p. 211) has identified as the capacity for agape love.

Are communes a threat to nuclear family life? The vast majority of communal groups throughout history have maintained family life in one form or another. Might there be situations where communal groups will weaken or dissolve nuclear families? Certainly, and the number of these groups and the restrictions they put on families will vary, based on the commune's ideology and use of commitment mechanisms. We know the Shaker's abolished family life, but they created a substitute for it. Communes have not replaced families, nor are they likely to in the future. Communes have and will be places which provide an alternative reality for family life. Just as cohabitation has not terminated the institution of marriage, communes will not supersede families.

The primary thesis of this book is that families are an essential component of communal life, unless a reliable substitute is found to replace them and their functions. As previously discussed, Hillery (1992) makes a convincing argument that although monasteries abolish families, agape love is substituted to compensate for part of their loss. Can communal family groups replace small nuclear families? In some cases yes, they can, and the Shakers as well as the Oneida Community are examples where this has happened. While the debate about whether nuclear families are destructive for communal living continues among scholars, this book has demonstrated that the answer to this question really is determined by the commune's ideology and organization.

The traditional or conventional argument about families and communes is basically a "lopsided view" of the problem (Shenker, 1986, p. 219). Barry Shenker believes, based on his study of the Hutterites and the Kibbutzim, that families have been a "contributory rather than a detrimental factor in the persistence" of these two groups and for many other communes too. The Hutterites and the Kibbutzim present a paradox for the conventional argument. In these two cases, and in others we have investigated such as Jesus People USA, "family recognition" and "community persistence" coincide with one another. According to Shenker (1986, p. 221), this is most evident regarding the issue of satisfaction. If one is satisfied in a variety of areas such as work, friendships, education, etc., one is more likely to become satisfied in other areas, according to Shenker. Satisfaction is contagious and spreads from one area to another. He recommends that for a community to persist, individuals "need to find balanced satisfaction." This can be achieved by balancing the affective satisfaction one obtains through family relationships, with the satisfaction one gains from being involved in community life. Ignoring either one of these dimensions of satisfaction hinders the development of the community and endangers the very survival of the community. Therefore, family relationships and their outcomes, such as affective satisfaction, can positively enhance community involvement rather than stifle it.

Community life is a series of trade-offs and checks and balances. Shenker (1986, p. 234) insists that successful communities, like the Hutterites and the Kibbutzim, have learned to meet each of the following needs of the community or the totality and those of the individual. If the following needs are not balanced, it can lead to the failure of communal life; totality-partiality, sharing-exclusiveness, dependence-independence, involvement-withdrawal, exposure-protection, and control-tolerance of deviance. The family, according to Shenker, assists communities in balancing these needs because it has certain "functional advantages," such as facilitating affective satisfaction, which influences the necessary balance and involvement of individuals in community life. If the balance is shifted in favor of the first item in each pair then the individual suffers, if more attention is directed to the second item in each pair then the community suffers. "A balanced situation is a sine qua non of community viability."

Some secondary theses of this book included: the role of communes as alternative lifestyles in comparison to traditional patterns of living, the influence of communal living on family life and intimate relationships, studying alternative families can give us insights into our own families and the status quo, and last but not least, studying communes provides us with concrete examples of how social order is created and sustained.

An even broader debate is raging regarding the nature of the modern American family and as Coontz (1997, p. 157) states,

> With 50% of American children living in something other than a married-couple family with both biological parents present, and with the tremendous variety of male and female responsibilities in today's different families, the time for abstract pronouncements about good or bad family structures and correct or incorrect parental roles is past. How a family functions is more important than its structure or its formal roles.

The concepts of structure and function are at the core of what traditional sociology is all about and they are at the center of the culture war over the family. Two fundamentally different assumptions or visions of moral authority, orthodoxy and progressivism, are at the center of the culture war or debate about the family. Those subscribing to the orthodox vision are usually cultural conservatives who believe the laws governing society and human social relations are eternal and unchanging. Truth is fixed. While progressivists usually support a more liberal or libertarian social agenda. They are more relativistic and for them, truth is not fixed, it is constantly evolving (Hunter, 1991).

Structures are social arrangements or how groups are organized, while functions are consequences of social arrangements that contribute to the overall stability of a system, organization, or group. While Coontz's position sounds convincing and applicable to communal life and families within communes, cultural conservatives and the new consensus group (otherwise referred to by Coontz as the conservative family values crusaders) would not find her argument at all convincing or accurate. Traditional marriage and a traditional style nuclear family structure are at the center of their mission to reinvigorate family life.

The Future of Communes

The 1990s is proving to be yet another significant period of growth in the history of communitarian development in the United States. Berry (1992, p. 245) argues that this growth can be attributed to the positive economic expansion the United States has experienced in the 1990s. The 15 years between 1975 and 1990 was a period of slow utopian development, but the communities that are being developed in the 1990s will be the leaders of a predicted surge in communitarian growth to occur in the next several years. The magnitude of this surge will be dependent on a variety of factors including; continued economic expansion, the appeal of communal living as a viable alternative to the nuclear family, the emotional as well as the structural health of the nuclear family, and whether those searching for nontraditional settings view communes as temporary way stations on their life's journey or as places where they are willing to make long-term commitments.

As the cost of living escalates, I expect, especially in urban areas, an increase in the number of people who will live in cooperatives and co-housing ventures. Sharing resources is one of the attractions of communal living and this becomes even more meaningful in an era of rising costs. I also anticipate that we will see an increase in the number of religious communes. The United States is still a country of religious seekers and because of this, people will continue to band together for spiritual purposes.

If communal history is an accurate predictor, it is likely that the majority of intentional communities in existence today will eventually dissolve. In a study conducted by Karen H. and G. Edward Stephan (1973) it was determined that of 143 communes founded between 1776 and 1900, nearly all of the secular communes dissolved within 10 years, while two thirds of the religious communes survived. One third of the religious communes lasted over 40 years. Communes where members practiced a single religious faith survived longer than those where more than one faith was being practiced. Stark (1998, p. 103) reports that only 3 of the 120 communes studied by Zablocki (1980) were in existence in 1997; two of the three were religious.

Those contemporary communes remaining will have successfully institutionalized the processes of commitment and conversion. Communal life, like family life, provides its adherents with mythical as well as real sustenance. There is something about these aspects of the human social condition that draws people to its life-giving qualities. Families dissolve, communities dissolve, and then these social groups rebuild again out of a searching for the challenges and the benefits that these arrangements provide.

Scholars have neglected the study of communal groups in the 1980s and 1990s. Communal living has frequently been dismissed as a fad that ended in the mid-1970s. Even researchers are influenced by "pop culture" and their interests shift to what is viewed as popular or chic. We need to push forward and study this fascinating and intriguing social phenomenon. One promising project is being conducted by Timothy Miller and Deborah Altus at the University of Kansas. They are in the process of collecting data on communities that existed in the United States between 1965 and 1975. I hope to continue my research by examining those contemporary communes which have identified family life as a specific focus of their group.

We need to find out what effects communal living had on the lives of former communalists, as well as the effects of communal living on those presently living in community. What influenced them to live in a communal setting? What attracted them to communal life and what has sustained them and kept them living in community? Are present day communalists living communally for the same reasons as those of the 1960s, 1970s, and 1980s? Are more of them ready to create "post-biological families?"

Additional research and theoretical work must be done concerning the survival of communes. Pitzer's (1997a) theoretical contribution of developmental communalism is an important start in the right direction. Oved (1993, p. 475) suggests that scholars should address and identify the important internal forces of survival in contemporary communes. Zablocki (1980, p. 357) encourages scholars to continue pursuing research concerning the social psychological components of charismatic relations and why people identify with charismatic leaders. I see a need for further research on evaluating how successful communal groups are in institutionalizing commitment. Sargent (1994, p. 16) suggests one of the problems researchers have encountered is the overemphasis in the literature with success, especially when it is measured in terms of longevity. More attention needs to be devoted to broadening our understanding of other possible meanings of success and ways of measuring it. Wagner (1983) provides a nonexhaustive list of seven criteria that could be used to evaluate communal groups.

The *Communities Directory* is a gold mine of potential leads for researchers. The communes listed in this guide are a collection of groups who have weathered many years of communal living, as well as those just getting started. Their members have chosen a lifestyle that is frequently viewed as deviant, but in reality is one that is mostly misunderstood and maligned. We have much to learn from these social experimenters and utopians as they attempt to create new social arrangements and search for meaning in their lives.

References

Abrams, Philip, & McCulloch, Andrew (1976). *Communes, sociology and society.* New York: Cambridge University Press.

Aidala, Angela A. (1983). Communes as seeking better family? A misleading explanation. *Alternative Lifestyles, 6,* 115-139.

Aidala, Angela A. (1989). Communes and changing family norms: Marriage and life-style choice among former members of communal groups. *Journal of Family Issues, 10,* 311-338.

Aidala, Angela A., & Zablocki, Benjamin D. (1991). Communes of the 1970s: Who joined and why? *Marriage and Family Review, 17,* 87-116.

Alam, Sterling E. (1978). Middle-class communes: The new surrogate extended family. In B. I. Murstein (Ed.), *Exploring intimate life styles* (pp. 82-107). New York: Springer.

Altman, Irwin, & Ginat, Joseph (1996). *Polygamous families in contemporary society.* New York: Cambridge University Press.

Andelson, Jonathan G. (1985a). The gift to be single: Celibacy and religious enthusiasm in the community of True Inspiration. *Communal Societies, 5,* 1-32.

Andelson, Jonathan G. (1985b). Living the mean: The ethos, practice, and genius of Amana. *Communities, 68,* 32-38.

Andelson, Jonathan G. (1997). The community of True Inspiration from Germany to the Amana colonies. In D. E. Pitzer (Ed.), *America's communal utopias* (pp. 181-203). Chapel Hill, NC: University of North Carolina Press.

Arndt, Karl J. R. (1997). George Rapp's harmony society. In D. E. Pitzer (Ed.), *America's communal utopias* (pp. 57-87). Chapel Hill, NC: University of North Carolina Press.

Bainbridge, William Sims (1997). *The sociology of religious movements.* London: Routledge & Kegan Paul.

Bane, Mary Jo (1976). *Here to stay: American families in the twentieth century.* New York: Basic Books.

Barkun, Michael (1984). Communal societies as cyclical phenomena. *Communal Societies, 4,* 35-48.

Barthel, Diane L. (1984). *Amana: From pietist sect to American community.* Lincoln, NE: University of Nebraska Press.

Barthel, Diane L. (1989). The American commune and the American mythology. *Qualitative Sociology, 12,* 241-260.

139

Bellah, Robert N., Madsen, Richard, Sullivan, William M., Swidler, Ann, & Tipton, Steven (1985). *Habits of the heart: Individualism and commitment in American life.* Berkeley, CA: University of California Press.

Bellah, Robert N., Madsen, Richard, Sullivan, William M., Swidler, Ann, & Tipton, Steven (1991). *The good society.* New York: Alfred A. Knopf.

Bennett, John W. (1975). Communes and communitarianism. *Theory and Society, 2,* 63-94.

Ben-Rafael, Eliezer (1997). *Crisis and transformation: The Kibbutz at century's end.* Albany, NY: State University of New York.

Berardo, Felix (1990). Trends and directions in family research in the 1980s. *Journal of Marriage and the Family, 52,* 809-817.

Berger, Bennett, Hackett, Bruce, & Millar, R. Mervyn (1972). The communal family. *The Family Coordinator, 21,* 419-427.

Berger, Bennett M. (1981). *The survival of a counterculture: Ideological work and everyday life among rural communards.* Berkeley, CA: University of California Press.

Berry, Brian J. L. (1992). *America's utopian experiments: Communal havens from long-wave crises.* Hanover, NH: University Press of New England.

Bouvard, Marguerite (1975). *The intentional community movement.* Port Washington, NY: Kennikat Press.

Bowes, A. M. (1989). *Kibbutz Goshen: An Israeli commune.* Prospect Heights, IL: Waveland Press.

Brewer, Priscilla J. (1986). *Shaker communities, Shaker lives.* Hanover, NH: University Press of New England.

Brewer, Priscilla J. (1997). The Shakers of Mother Ann Lee. In Donald E. Pitzer (Ed.), *America's communal utopias* (pp. 37-56). Chapel Hill, NC: University of North Carolina Press.

Bromley, David G., & Shupe, Anson D. (1981). *Strange gods: The great American cult scare.* Boston: Beacon Press.

Brudenell, Gerry. (1983). Radical community: Contemporary communes and intentional communities. In Eleanor D. Macklin, & Roger H. Rubin (Eds.), *Contemporary families and alternative lifestyles: Handbook on research and theory* (pp. 235-255). Beverly Hills, CA: Sage.

Carden, Maren Lockwood (1971). *Oneida: Utopian community to modern corporation.* New York: Harper Torchbooks.

Cavan, Ruth. (1976). Communes: Historical and contemporary. *International Review of Modern Sociology, 6,* 1-11.

Conover, Patrick W. (1978). Communes and intentional communities. *Journal of Voluntary Action Research, 7,* 5-17.

Constantine, Larry L., & Constantine, J. M. (1973). *Group marriage: A study of contemporary multilateral marriage.* New York: Macmillan.

Constantine, Larry L. (1977). Where are the kids? Children in alternative life-styles. In Robert W. Libby, & Robert N. Whitehurst (Eds.), *Marriage and alternatives: Exploring intimate relationships* (pp. 257-263). Glenview, IL: Scott, Foresman.

Coontz, Stephanie (1992). *The way we never were: American families and the nostalgia trap.* New York: Basic Books.

Coontz, Stephanie (1997). *The way we really are: Coming to terms with America's changing families.* New York: Basic Books.

Cornfield, Noreen (1983). The success of urban communes. *Journal of Marriage and Family, 45,* 115-126.

Criden, Yosef, & Gelb, Saadia (1976). *The Kibbutz experience: Dialogue in Kfar Blum.* New York: Schocken Books.

Daner, Francine Jeanne (1976). *The American children of Krsna: A study of the Hare Krsna movement.* New York: Holt, Rinehart and Winston.

dePilis, Mario S. (1985). Early Mormon communitarianism. *Communities, 68,* 39-42.

Durnbaugh, Donald (1997). Communitarian societies in colonial America. In Donald E. Pitzer (Ed.), *America's communal utopias* (pp. 14-36). Chapel Hill, NC: University of North Carolina Press.

Ebaugh, Helen Rose Fuchs. (1993). *Women in the vanishing cloister: Organizational decline in Catholic religious orders in the United States.* New Brunswick, NJ: Rutgers University Press.

Eshleman, J. Ross (1997). *The family.* Boston: Allyn and Bacon.

Etzioni, Amitai (1996). The responsive community: A communitarian perspective. *American Sociological Review, 61,* 1-11.

Fairfield, Richard (1972). *Communes USA: A personal tour.* Baltimore: Penguin Books.

Fellowship for Intentional Community (1995). *Communities directory: A guide to cooperative living.* Langley, WA: Fellowship for Intentional Community.

Ferrar, Kshama (1982). Experiences of parents in contemporary communal households. *Alternative Lifestyles, 5,* 7-23.

Fogarty, Robert S. (1990). *All things new: American communes and utopian movements 1860-1914.* Chicago: University of Chicago Press.

Gauthier, Monique (Producer). (1992). *Follow the dirt road: An introduction to intentional communities in the 1990s* (Videocassette, 53 minutes).

Foster, Lawrence (1981). *Religion and sexuality: Three American communal experiments of the nineteenth century.* New York: Oxford University Press.

Foster, Lawrence (1988). The rise and fall of utopia: The Oneida Community of 1852 and 1879. *Communal Societies, 8,* 1-17.

Foster, Lawrence (1991). *Women, family, and utopia: Communal experiments of the Shakers, the Oneida Community, and the Mormons.* Syracuse, NY: Syracuse University Press.

Foster, Lawrence (1997). Free love and community: John Humphrey Noyes and the Oneida perfectionists. In Donald E. Pitzer (Ed.), *America's communal utopias* (pp. 253-278). Chapel Hill, NC: University of North Carolina Press.

Galanter, Marc (1989). *Cults: Faith, healing, and coercion.* New York: Oxford University Press.

Gardner, Hugh (1978). *The children of prosperity: Thirteen modern American communes.* New York: St. Martin's Press.

Grossmann, Walter (1984). The origins of the True Inspired of Amana. *Communal Societies, 4,* 133-149.

Guarneri, Carl J. (1997). Brook farm and the fourierist phalanxes. In Donald E. Pitzer (Ed.), *America's communal utopias* (pp. 159-180). Chapel Hill, NC: University of North Carolina Press.

Hall, John R. (1978). *The ways out: Utopian communal groups in an age of Babylon.* London: Routledge and Kegan Paul.

Hall, John R. (1988). Social organization and pathways of commitment: Types of communal groups, rational choice theory, and the Kanter thesis. *American Sociological Review, 53,* 679-692.

Hall, John R. (1990). The apocalypse at Jonestown. In Thomas Robbins, & Dick Anthony (Eds.), *In gods we trust: New patterns of religious pluralism in America* (pp. 269-293). New Brunswick, NJ: Transaction Publishers.

Hassinger, Edward W., & Pinkerton, James R. (1986). *The human community.* New York: Macmillan.

Hertz, Rosanna (1982). Family in the Kibbutz: A review of authority relations and women's status. In Harriet Gross, & Marvin B. Sussman (Eds.), *Alternatives to traditional family living* (Vol. 5). *Marriage & Family Review,* New York: Haworth Press.

Hillery, George (1992). *The monastery: A study in freedom, love, and community.* Westport, CT: Praeger.

Horgan, Edward. R. (1987). *The Shaker holy land: A community portrait.* Boston: Harvard Common Press.

Hostetler, John A. (1977). *Hutterite society.* Baltimore: Johns Hopkins University Press.

Hostetler, John A., & Huntington, Gertrude Enders (1996). *The Hutterites in North America.* Orlando, FL: Harcourt Brace.

Hunter, James Davison (1991). *Culture wars: The struggle to define America.* New York: Basic Books.

Huntington, Gertrude E. (1997). Living in the Aak: Four centuries of Hutterite faith and community. In Donald E. Pitzer (Ed.), *America's communal utopias* (pp. 319-351). Chapel Hill, NC: University of North Carolina Press.

Janzen, Rod (1994). The Prairieleut: A forgotten Hutterite people. *Communal Societies,* 14, 67-89.

Jerome, Judson (1974). *Families of Eden: Communes and the new anarchism.* New York: Seabury Press.

Johnston, Charley M., & Deisher, Robert W. (1973). Contemporary communal child rearing: A first analysis. *Pediatrics, 52,* 319-326.

Kain, Edward L. (1990). *The myth of family decline: Understanding families in a world of rapid social change.* Lexington, MA: Lexington Books.

Kanter, Rosabeth Moss (1972). *Commitment and community: Communes and utopias in sociological perspective.* Cambridge, MA: Harvard University Press.

Kanter, Rosabeth Moss (Ed.). (1973a). *Communes creating and managing the collective life.* New York: Harper and Row Publishers.

Kanter, Rosabeth Moss, & Halter, Marilyn (1973b). *De-housewifing women, domesticating men: Changing sex roles in urban communes.* Paper presented at the annual meeting of the American Psychological Association, Montreal.

Kanter, Rosabeth Moss (1977). The new utopian vision? Bringing community to the family. *Journal of Current Social Issues, 14,* 76-81.

Kanter, Rosabeth Moss (1979). Communes in cities. In John Case, & Rosemary C. R. Taylor (Eds.), *Co-ops, communes & collectives: Experiments in social change in the 1960s and 1970s* (pp. 112-135). New York: Pantheon Books.

Kaslow, Florence, & Sussman, Marvin B. (Eds.). (1982). Cults and the family. *Marriage & Family Review, 4,* 1-192. New York: Haworth Press.

Kephart, William M. (1982). *Extraordinary groups: The sociology of unconventional life-styles.* New York: St. Martin's Press.

Kephart, William M. (1987). *Extraordinary groups: An examination of unconventional life-styles* (Rev. ed.). New York: St. Martin's Press.

Kephart, William M., & Zellner, William W. (1991). *Extraordinary groups: An examination of unconventional life-styles* (Rev. ed.). New York: St. Martin's Press.

Kephart, William M., & Zellner, William W. (1994). *Extraordinary groups: An examination of unconventional life-styles* (Rev. ed.) New York: St. Martin's Press.

Kern, Louis J. (1981). *An ordered love: Sex roles and sexuality in victorian utopias—The Shakers, the Mormons, and the Oneida Community.* Chapel Hill, NC: University of North Carolina Press.

Kinkade, Kathleen (1973). *A Walden Two experiment: The first five years of Twin Oaks Community.* New York: William Morrow and Company.

Kinkade, Kathleen (1994). *Is it utopia yet?: An insider's view of Twin Oaks Community in its twenty-sixth year.* Louisa, VA: Twin Oaks Publishing.

Klee-Hartzell, Marlyn (1996). The Oneida Community family. *Communal Societies, 16,* 15-22.

Komar, Ingrid (1983). *Living the dream: A documentary study of the Twin Oaks Community.* Norwood, PA: Norwood Editions.

Kozeny, Geoph (1995). Intentional communities: Lifestyles based on ideals. *Communities directory: A guide to cooperative living* (pp. 18-24). Langley, WA: Fellowship for Intentional Community.

Lasch, Christopher (1979). *Haven in a heartless world: The family besieged.* New York: Basic Books.

Latkin, Carl A., Sundberg, Norman D., Littman, Richard A., Katsikis, Melissa G., & Hagan, Richard A. (1994). Feelings after the fall: Former Rajneeshpuram commune members' perceptions of and affiliation with the Rajneeshee movement. *Sociology of Religion, 55,* 65-73.

Lauer, Jeannette C., & Lauer, Robert H. (1983a). Sex roles in nineteenth century American communal societies. *Communal Societies, 3,* 16-28.

Lauer, Robert H., & Lauer, Jeanette C. (1983b). *The spirit and the flesh: Sex in utopian communities.* Metuchen, NJ: Scarecrow Press.

Lee, S. C., & Brattrud, Audrey (1967). Marriage under a monastic mode of life: A preliminary report on the Hutterite family in South Dakota. *Journal of Marriage and the Family, 29,* 512-520.

Levine, Saul V., Carr, Robert P., & Horenblas, Wendy (1973). The urban commune: Fact or fad, promise or pipedream? *American Journal of Orthopsychiatry, 43,* 149-163.

Levitas, Ruth (1990). *The concept of utopia.* Syracuse, NY: Syracuse University Press.

Macklin, Eleanor D. (1980). Nontraditional family forms: A decade of research. *Journal of Marriage and the Family, 42,* 175-192.

Mannheim, Karl (1936). *Ideology and utopia: An introduction to the sociology of knowledge.* New York: Harcourt Brace Jovanovich.

May, Dean L. (1997). One heart and mind: Communal life and values among the Mormons. In Donald E. Pitzer (Ed.), *America's communal utopias* (pp. 135-158). Chapel Hill, NC: University of North Carolina Press.

McNamara, Jo Ann Kay (1996). *Sisters in arms: Catholic nuns through two millennia.* Cambridge: Harvard University Press.

McCrank, Lawrence J. (1997). Religious orders and monastic communalism in America. In Donald E. Pitzer (Ed.), *America's communal utopias* (pp. 204-252). Chapel Hill, NC: University of North Carolina Press.

McCord, William (1989). *Voyages to utopia: From monastery to commune the search for the perfect society.* New York: W. W. Norton.

McLoughlin, William G. (1978). *Revivals, awakenings, and reform: An essay on religion and social change in America, 1607-1977.* Chicago: University of Chicago Press.

Melnyk, George (1985). *From utopia to a co-operative society.* Montreal: Black Rose Books.

Melton, J. Gordon (1992). *Encyclopedic handbook of cults in America.* New York: Garland Publishing.

Melton, J. Gordon, & Moore, Robert L. (1982). *The cult experience: Responding to the new religious pluralism.* New York: Pilgrim Press.

Miller, Timothy (Ed.). (1990). *American communes, 1860-1960: A bibliography.* New York: Garland.

Miller, Timothy. (Ed.). (1991). *When prophets die: The postcharismatic fate of new religious movements.* Albany, NY: State University of New York Press.

Miller, Timothy (1992a). *The evolution of hippie communal spirituality.* Paper presented at the annual meeting of the American Academy of Religion, San Francisco.

Miller, Timothy (1992b). The roots of the 1960s communal revival. *American Studies, 33,* 73-93.

Miller, Timothy (Ed.). (1995). *America's alternative religions.* Albany, NY: State University of New York Press.

Minturn, Leigh (1984). Sex-role differentiation in contemporary communes. *Sex Roles, 10,* 73-85.

Mowery, Jeni (1978). Systemic requisites of communal groups. *Alternative Lifestyles, 1,* 235-261.

Muncy, Raymond Lee (1973). *Sex and marriage in utopian communities: 19th century America.* Bloomington, IN: Indiana University Press.

Murnstein, Bernard (Ed.). (1978). *Exploring intimate life styles.* New York: Springer.

Nisbet, Robert A. (1966). *The sociological tradition.* New York: Basic Books.

Niv, Amittai (1980). Organizational disintegration: Roots, processes, and types. In John R. Kimberly, Robert H. Miles, & Associates (Eds.), *The organizational life cycle* (pp. 375-394). San Francisco: Jossey-Bass Publishers.

Norris, Kathleen (1996). *The cloister walk.* New York: Riverhead Books.

Ogilvy, Jay, & Ogilvy, Heather (1972). Communes and the reconstruction of reality. In Sallie TeSelle (Ed.), *The family, communes, and utopian societies* (pp. 83-99). New York: Harper Torchbooks.

Okugawa, Oto (1980). Annotated list of communal and utopian societies, 1787-1919. In Robert S. Fogarty (Ed.), *Dictionary of American communal and utopian history* (pp. 172-233). Westport, CT: Greenwood Press.

Oved, Yaacov (1993). *Two hundred years of American communes.* New Brunswick, NJ: Transaction Publishers.

Palmer, Susan Jean (1994). *Moon sisters, Krishna mothers, Rajneesh lovers: Women's roles in new religions.* Syracuse, NY: Syracuse University Press.

Parsons, Arthur S. (1985). Redemptory intimacy: The family culture of the unification church. *Communal Societies, 5,* 137-175.

Peter, Karl A. (1987). *The dynamics of Hutterite society: An analytical approach.* Edmonton: University of Alberta Press.

Pfaffenberger, Bryan (1982). A world of husbands and mothers: Sex roles and their ideological context in the formation of the farm. In Jon Wagner (Ed.), *Sex roles in contemporary American communes* (pp. 172-210). Bloomington, IN: Indiana University Press.

Pitzer, Donald E. (1984a). *The uses of the American communal past.* Keynote address for the tenth annual Historic Communal Societies conference, New Harmony, IN, October 13, 1983. *Communal Societies, 4,* 215-242.

Pitzer, Donald E. (1984b). Collectivism, community and commitment: America's religious communal utopias from the Shakers to Jonestown. In Peter Alexander, & Roger Gill (Eds.), *Utopias* (pp. 119-135). London: Gerald Duckworth.

Pitzer, Donald E. (1989). Developmental communalism: An alternative approach to communal studies. In Dennis Hardy, & Lorna Davidson (Eds.), *Utopian thought and communal experience* (pp. 68-76). Geography and Planning Paper No. 24. Middlesex Polytechnic.

Pitzer, Donald E. (Ed.). (1997a). *America's communal utopias*. Chapel Hill, NC: University of North Carolina Press.

Pitzer, Donald E. (1997b). The new moral world of Robert Owen and New Harmony. In Donald E. Pitzer Ed., *America's communal utopias* (pp. 88-134). Chapel Hill, NC: University of North Carolina Press.

Popenoe, David (1993a). Point of View. *The Chronicle of Higher Education, 39,* (April 14) A48.

Popenoe, David (1993b). American family decline, 1960-1990: A review and appraisal. *Journal of Marriage and the Family, 55,* 527-555.

Procter-Smith, Majorie (1985). *Women in Shaker community and worship*. Lewiston, NY: Edwin Mellen Press.

Questenberry, Dan, & Deer Rock (1995). Who we are: An explanation of what 'intentional community' means. *Communities directory: A guide to cooperative living* (pp. 33-38). Langley, WA: Fellowship for Intentional Community.

Ramey, James W. (1978). Life styles of the future. In Bernard Murstein (Ed.), *Exploring intimate life styles* (pp. 274-286). New York: Springer Publishing.

Reiss, Ira L. (1980). *Family systems in America*. New York: Holt, Rinehart and Winston.

Rigby, Andrew (1974). *Alternative realities: A study of communes and their members*. London: Routledge & Kegan Paul.

Roberts, Ron (1971). *The new communes: Coming together in America*. Englewood Cliffs, NJ: Prentice-Hall.

Robbins, Thomas (1988). *Cults, converts, and charisma: The sociology of new religious movements*. London: Sage.

Rochford, E. Burke (1985). *Hare Krishna in America*. New Brunswick, NJ: Rutgers University Press.

Rochford, E. Burke (1995). Family structure, commitment, and involvement in the Hare Krishna movement. *Sociology of Religion, 56,* 153-175.

Rubin, Roger (1983). Epilogue: Families and alternative lifestyles in an age of technological revolution. In Eleanor D. Macklin, & H. Rubin (Eds.), *Contemporary families and alternative lifestyles: Handbook on research and theory* (pp. 400-409). Beverly Hills, CA: Sage.

Ruth, David J. (1978). The commune movement in the middle 1970s. In Bernard I. Murstein (Ed.), *Exploring intimate life styles* (pp. 69-81). New York: Springer Publishing.

Sargent, Lyman T. (1994). The three faces of utopianism revisited. *Utopian Studies, 5,* 1-37.

Schulterbrandt, Joy G., & Nichols, Edwin J. (1972). Ethical and ideological problems for communal living: A caveat. *The Family Coordinator, 21,* 429-433.

Shambaugh, Bertha M. H. (1988). *Amana: The community of True Inspiration*. Iowa City, IA: Penfield Press.

Shenker, Barry. (1986). *Intentional communities: Ideology and alienation in communal societies*. London: Routledge & Kegan Paul.

Shey, Thomas H. (1977). Why communes fail: A comparative analysis of the viability of Danish and American communes. *Journal of Marriage and the Family, 39*, 605-613.

Shinn, Larry D. (1987). *The dark Lord: Cult images and the Hare Krishnas in America.* Philadelphia: Westminster Press.

Skinner, B. F. (1948). *Walden Two.* New York: Macmillan.

Skolnick, Arlene (1991). *Embattled paradise: The American family in an age of uncertainty.* New York: Basic Books.

Slater, Philip (1970). *The pursuit of loneliness.* Boston: Beacon Press.

Smith, William L. (1984). *Urban communitarianism in the 1980s: Seven religious communes in Chicago.* (Unpublished doctoral dissertation, University of Notre Dame, IN.

Smith, William L. (1986). The use of structural arrangements and organizational strategies by urban communes. *Communal Societies, 6,* 118-137.

Smith, William L. (1991). Recent changes in Hutterite colony expansion. *The Great Plains Sociologist, 4,* 63-67.

Smith, William L. (1992). The world of meaning of urban religious communalists. *SYZYGY: Journal of Alternative Religion and Culture, 1,* 137-146.

Smith, William L. (1994). The impact of communal living on children in the 1980s. *SYZYGY: Journal of Alternative Religion and Culture, 3,* 51-60.

Smith, William L. (1996a). The contemporary communal movement. In Dan A. Chekki (Ed.), *Research in community sociology, Vol. 6* (pp. 239-261). Greenwich, CT: JAI Press.

Smith, William L. (1996b). Are the old order Amish becoming more like the Hutterites? *Michigan Sociological Review, 10,* 68-86.

Spiro, Melford E. (1972). *Venture in utopia.* New York: Schocken Books.

Stacey, Judith (1990). *Brave new families.* New York: Basic Books.

Stark, Rodney (1998). *Sociology.* Belmont, CA: Wadsworth Publishing.

Stark, Rodney, & Bainbridge, William Sims (1985). *The future of religion: Secularization, revival, and cult formation.* Berkeley, CA: University of California Press.

Stein, Maurice (1960). *The eclipse of community.* Princeton, NJ: Princeton University Press.

Stein, Stephen J. (1992). *The Shaker experience in America: A history of the United Society of Believers.* New Haven, CT: Yale University Press.

Stephan, Karen H., & Stephan, G. Edward (1973). Religion and the survival of utopian communities. *Journal for the Scientific Study of Religion, 12,* 89-100.

Sturm, Douglas (1972). The Kibbutzim and the spirit of Israel: An interpretive essay. In Sallie TeSelle (Ed.), *The family, communes, and utopian societies* (pp. 100-120). New York: Harper Torchbooks.

Sutton, Robert P. (1997). An American elysium: The Icarian communities. In Donald E. Pitzer (Ed.), *America's communal utopias* (pp. 279-296). Chapel Hill, NC: University of North Carolina Press.

Talmon, Yonina (1973). Family life in the Kibbutz: From revolutionary days to stabilization. In Rosabeth Moss Kanter (Ed.), *Communes: Creating and managing the collective life* (pp. 318-333). New York: Harper and Row.

Veysey, Laurence (1978). *The communal experience: Anarchist & mystical communities in twentieth-century America.* Chicago: University of Chicago Press.

Wagner, Jon (Ed.). (1982a). *Sex roles in contemporary American communes.* Bloomington, IN: Indiana University Press.

Wagner, Jon (1982b). Sex roles in American communal utopias: An overview. In Jon Wagner (Ed.), *Sex roles in contemporary American communes* (pp. 1-44). Bloomington, IN: Indiana University Press.

Wagner, Jon (1985). Success in intentional communities: The problem of evaluation. *Communal Societies, 5,* 89-100.

Wagner, Jon (1986). Sexuality and gender roles in utopian communities: A critical survey of scholarly work. *Communal Societies, 6,* 172-188.

Wagner, Jon (1997). Eric Jansson and the Bishop Hill Colony. In Donald E. Pitzer (Ed.), *America's communal utopias* (pp. 297-318). Chapel Hill, NC: University of North Carolina Press.

Wayland-Smith, Ellen (1988). The status and self-perception of women in the Oneida community. *Communal Societies, 8,* 18-53.

Weisner, Thomas S., & Martin, Joan C. (1979). Learning environments for infants: Communes and conventionally married families in California. *Alternative Lifestyles, 2,* 201-242.

Whitworth, John McKelvie (1975). *God's blueprints: A sociological study of three utopian sects.* London: Routledge & Kegan Paul.

Wittberg, Patricia (1994). *The rise and decline of Catholic religious orders: A social movement perspective.* Albany, NY: State University of New York Press.

Yinger, J. Milton (1982). *Countercultures: The promise and peril of a world turned upside down.* New York: Free Press.

Zablocki, Benjamin (1971). *The joyful community.* Baltimore: Penguin Books.

Zablocki, Benjamin (1980). *Alienation and charisma: A study of contemporary American communes.* New York: Free Press.

Zicklin, Gilbert (1983). *Countercultural communes: A sociological perspective.* Westport, CT: Greenwood Press.

Author Index

Subject Index

About the Author

William L. Smith is Associate Professor of Sociology in the Department of Sociology and Anthropology at Georgia Southern University. He received his PhD from the University of Notre Dame. His research and teaching interests include family, community, race and ethnicity, and religion. He has written a variety of articles and book chapters on such topics as pedagogy, new religious movements, communal life, racial and ethnic relations, family studies, and Irish priests. He is presently engaged in projects on Irish priests, families in contemporary communes, and ethnic parishes, and is currently a reviewer and a former member of the editorial board of the quarterly journal, *Teaching Sociology*.